Adrian Mark Dore

Economic Injustice

What A Screw-Up

First published in 2019

VALUE CREATION PRESS
Bristol
Somerset
United Kingdom
valuecreationpress.co.uk
info@valuecreationpress.co.uk

ISBN: 978-0-9555178-2-2

Contents

Preface

Does economic injustice affect you?
Yes, unquestionably.

Will, what's said in this book impact on you?
Yes, unquestionably.

Why? Because, our economy affects every facet of life - social, environmental and economic. We all have a different perspective of the world - different things concern us. However, all these different concerns have a common underlying cause - our economy. When the economy is imbalanced, as it is now, it causes an adverse ripple effect throughout life. Your concerns, whatever they are, are linked to this imbalanced economy. You are **NOT** going to address these concerns effectively until you address what's causing them - an imbalanced economy.

Why is our economy imbalanced? The wealthy one per cent have hijacked it to serve their needs, not ours. This has created the imbalance. This is not how a democracy is supposed to work. The economy is supposed to serve the needs of the majority. It's supposed to be balanced. This imbalance is an injustice, as our economy only serves the needs of a few, and therefore, it's a screw-up.

Over the past forty years, the wealthy one per cent have manipulated the economy, changing laws and regulations, and introducing practices and procedures to serve their needs. I will explain what they've done, how it's hurting you, and how together, we can change it - to get things to work for us. To provide balance to the economy, and life.

It's written in an easy to follow, non-technical way so all can understand, as it affects ninety-nine per cent of us. Collectively we have the power to bring about democratic change. To get the economy to work for us, not against us. Unless we raise our voice in protest and demand change, we will continue our downward slide to who knows where?

If you want to make a real difference, then you need to understand what economic issues underlie your problems. Only with this knowledge and understanding can you make a difference by calling on government to take specific action. Change does not occur through vague demands. It only happens when one is specific about a problem and its solution. Therefore, this book provides an important first step in helping you understand what's really causing the problems which concern you. You can then be specific in calling for action and getting much-needed change.

It's also important that you see your problem in the correct context. For example, plastic pollution may be a concern of yours, and you think that by calling on the government to stop its use, is the answer. What about other types of pollution and bad environmental practices, are they allowed to continue? The problems of business pollution are part of a wider issue of how we see and manage business. We have to understand this context, to be able to address not only plastics but much broader concerns. So, rather than taking off on a tangent "to solve the plastics problem" you need to understand this context - to see that if we address the real cause, yours and many other problems are also rectified. This book will help put all these pieces together simply and easily.

The wealthy one per cent will not take these changes lying down. They are powerful and influential; that's why change will only happen through mass awareness and action. It starts with you reading this book – spreading the word and joining others in calling for change. It's your future at stake. Unless you shape the future others will, just as they have done over the past four decades, to your disadvantage.

Introduction

Free market economics has dictated economic life for the past forty years. I'm sure you've heard the terms "free markets" and "globalisation." No doubt in a positive context, as we've been browbeaten into believing they're an essential part of a modern, thriving economy. However, the concept, including its name - "free market", is misleading. Rather than free our economy, it has trapped us. It has trapped us in a world of increasing economic inequality and insecurity, creating huge social problems. It has led to harmful and unsustainable practices, causing extensive environmental damage. Therefore, a more fitting name for "free market economics" would be "enslavement economics." Enslaving the majority through the practices, procedures and systems of a few. Another apt name would be "apartheid economics" - an economy serving the needs of a few while excluding the majority.

Free markets and globalisation are only the tips of the iceberg. The extent of economic manipulation is vast, adversely affecting every facet of our economy. Through a continuous stream of disinformation, falsehoods, half-truths, and obfuscation, together with political extortion and manipulation, a small group of vested interests have been able to hoodwink us into believing what they are doing is in our interests. Nothing is further from the truth. They are knowingly inflicting harm in pursuit of self-enrichment, which is malicious. We have reached breaking point where we can continue no longer. We need to change the rules of our economy. We need a new set of rules and systems, ones which serve the many, not the few.

Let's be clear, we are not trying to change the immutable laws of nature, or physics, but man-made laws, practices, procedures and policies introduced over the past forty years to serve this small minority. Economist around the world now agree, inequality (or injustice) is not due to any economic law, but of our own design and making. They are of the opinion it's a design failure. I disagree. It's not a design failure, but one of deliberate design and manipulation to serve the wealthy one per cent. Once you are aware of these manipulations, you can add your voice to those calling for change. Collectively, we can make a difference.

However, we are up against powerful and influential interests, but they are no match against mass calls for reform.

We now estimate that the top one per cent globally, own as much wealth as the remaining ninety-nine per cent. With this economic power comes political power. This power and influence does not end with political manipulation - it's pervasive in every respect. They use it to influence regulatory bodies, institutions representing business professions, the media - absolutely every entity which will further their cause or hinder it. They use their power to manipulate outcomes to serve their needs. They couch these manipulations in a manner and language which claims to serve the needs of the majority, when it does nothing of the sort. They then work hard at convincing us that alternate solutions are impossible, that doing things differently will inevitably harm us.

The wealthy one per cent banked on no mass involvement because that's the message they have promoted. "These are technical matters beyond the masses understanding." Like all the things they have told us - that's simply untrue. What I will explain is straightforward and simple. Written for the person feeling the economic pinch, or concerned about the effects of poor economic policies. For those unsure what's causing the problems, and even less sure of what to do about it.

Our Economic Screw-Up
results from over forty years of vested interest developing practices, procedures, policies and systems to serve their needs, not ours. Their manipulative practices have worked well for them. Economic inequality is growing rapidly, and set to grow even faster in the coming years. Our economy is seriously imbalanced. No imbalanced system can sustain itself for long. It will crash and burn, but such an outcome serves nobodies interests. Avarice has blinded the one per cent, yet some of them realise it has gone too far, and needs to be brought back under control, where wealth is distributed more evenly. It's now our turn to unravel this dysfunctional system; to replace it with new, fair and effective systems. This is not somebody else's problem. It's a problem we must address together, by speaking out and taking action where we can, based on a clear understanding of the problems. It's only

through our collective demands that we can bring about change. The catalyst for change will not come from the government, economists, business and definitely not from the wealthy one per cent. It will only come from those who bear the brunt of economic inequality - the ninety-nine per cent of us. We have the power to change things but only if we act collectively to influence government action.

Hiding the truth by confusing and misleading us.
When we challenge the regulations, practices, procedures, policies and systems employed in our economy today, accusing them of being the source of our problems, vested interest responds by claiming our standard-of-living has improved, and therefore, we have little to complain about. It's true, the average person's standard-of-living has improved over the past four decades (as most benefit from today's modern products and services,) but our quality-of-life has not. Neither has our environment fared well. It's not just about improving our standard-of-living (although important), but also ensuring a high quality-of-life while protecting the environment.

So, parts of what they are doing are good at improving our standard-of-living; coming up with innovative products and services. We don't want to lose this, so we don't want to "throw the baby away with the bathwater." We need to keep what's good and change what's bad.

For a long time, many of us have felt unease about what's going on around us. We see great affluence, but also poverty and suffering. Life generally is getting tougher for middle and lower income groups. It's been getting progressively worse over the past four decades. The environment is also paying the price for our greed. Something is wrong, but what precisely? Most blame Capitalism for these problems, but it's a popular myth that vested interests want to maintain and promote, as it's a smokescreen hiding the real cause of our problems. Capitalism is an ideology; it's not a law, practice, procedure or system which is propping up our current, unfair and broken economic system. It's these unfair laws, practices, procedures and systems introduced by vested interests over decades, which we need to dismantle, not Capitalism.

Capitalism is an ideology. As with any ideology, it's difficult to be precise in identifying problems as it represents ideas, not practices, procedures or systems. It's these practices, procedures and systems we use every day, which are at the heart of our problems, not vague ideas or principles. Vested interests want people to waste their time chasing vague ideas because it's difficult to introduce any meaningful change by accusing an ideology of our problems. However, if we identify genuine bad practices, procedures or systems and change them - that's what will bring about a meaningful change. They don't want their bad practices found out. They don't want the systems they have developed over decades, which intentionally manipulate the economy to serve their needs, uncovered. However, that's precisely what we will do in this book; peel back all the misleading information spread to confuse us, to reveal the truth about our economy.

Capitalism embodies the principles of free enterprise, which is the most effective way of improving our standard-of-living and quality-of-life. Free enterprise is not the principle responsible for creating economic inequality, or for destroying the environment. Therefore, I support keeping Capitalism but changing how we implement it. Free enterprise is the baby we don't want to throw away with the bathwater. Capitalism can work for the good of all if we change our current bad systems, practices and procedures. It's all possible, as this book will explain.

Business must become a social tool, a way to uplift and benefit all. It can no longer remain the means to enrich a few, at the cost of the many, and our environment. We want and need business to succeed and grow, but not at the expense of others. For a business to succeed and grow, it must make a profit, as shareholders, like others involved in the business, must be fairly and justly rewarded for their endeavours. If a business does not make a profit over the long-term, it fails, and we as a society lose the means to support and uplift ourselves. So, the profit objective and making money is not our enemy, but rather crucial elements for growth and development. Capitalism, free enterprise and profit are valuable concepts, provided we do not lose sight of the end goal and end up chasing profit instead. Profit is only a means to an end. The object is to improve the standard-of-living and quality-of-life for all while also protecting our environment. Together, by making the necessary changes recommended in this book, we can achieve this. We can achieve a balanced, equitable economy serving the needs of all.

The extent of the manipulation.

Throughout this book, you will be introduced to the extent vested interests have gone to mislead us. To cover up and hide the problems they have caused. These problems are now becoming so large they are finding it more difficult to hide. You hear on a regular basis the problems caused by austerity programmes, of stagnant wages, increasing poverty in developed economies, pollution, environmental degradation. However, a large number still remain well hidden from you. Most people are not aware of the extent of economic inequality, and neither do they appreciate its harmful effects. They also underestimate their role and that of the government in rectifying the problems. This is what vested interests want. They want people to remain in the dark, because otherwise they will become angry and demand the government make changes, which they can. People do not realise the extent to which they have been manipulated. This book will expose these manipulations.

As already explained, we cannot expect change to come from government, economists, investors, businesspeople or accountants. These are bodies or professions adversely influenced and deeply entwined in the problems. They represent the interests of the one per cent. They will not change. Change will only come from you and I, those in the middle/lower income groups. Those most adversely affected. We make up ninety-nine per cent of the population, so we have considerable power if we act collectively. We must be the catalyst for change. We must get the government to implement much-needed change. Only by raising our voices in protest and calling for change can we achieve this. Matters will only get worse if we don't take action.

It's frightening to think how the influence and power of a small group (the wealthy one per cent) can sway the democratic process in their favour. Surely, being in the majority, our needs should be served, not those of a small minority? Unfortunately, it's no longer "one person one vote" but "one buck one vote." This is economic apartheid, and it's found in all developed economies even in countries like the UK who place strict limits on electoral funding. Money buys political influence - that's a fact we have to live with. Those with wealth use it to strengthen their political and economic position. They use their power to reshape our thinking, to make palatable the unpalatable. They control the media - the messages we hear, and therefore public perception. They feed us a message that serves their needs. They do this relentlessly until people accept the message as fact.

The world abhorred political apartheid as practised in South Africa in the past, but what's the difference between it and economic apartheid? The end result is the same - the needs of the majority are not served but rather those of a tiny minority. Economic apartheid must be ended just as the world put pressure on South Africa to end political apartheid. Economic apartheid has been hurting the majority for far too long - time to question all, and to make changes.

How this book addresses our economic problems.
The wealthy one per cent have manipulated our economy by introducing laws, regulations, practices, procedures and systems to serve their interests. By identifying these, and getting them changed, we start rolling back their control over the economy.

We must be specific in targeting problems as then our actions can be specific. Being vague, like blaming an ideology, means nothing changes, as we have failed to be specific in identifying a cause and its symptoms. Importantly, we should be clear on identifying a solution. Identifying problems alone doesn't leave us much better off. Finding a solution is the only way to improve our situation. I will describe our problems and their solutions. Some, we must implement now, while others may take a little longer. As long as we know of the problems and working towards changing them, that's what matters. We need to take positive and meaningful steps to implement change now – that's what's critically important. Your involvement and that of your colleagues, friends and family is what will make all the difference. As individuals, we have no chance of bringing about change. It's all about collective action - standing together and using our ninety-nine votes against one to bring about change.

Every chapter introduces at least one or more problems. These represent the major problems we face, not all. I explain the problems and their solutions in a simple, logical way. I could describe each problem in greater detail, but the idea is only to provide sufficient understanding of the problem and its solution. To provide enough information so you can stop the spread of misleading information, falsehoods, half-truths, disinformation and obfuscation, and hold vested interest accountable for what they are really up to. The truth will hurt them if we stand together and call for change by having a basic understanding of the problems and their solutions.

Below is a very brief introduction to each chapter and the problems they address. You don't have to read all chapters, they stand independently. However, it would be beneficial if you read the entire book - each chapter is important. Although each chapter addresses a unique problem(s), the reality is they are all intertwined.

Chapter 1
Replace our inadequate and inappropriate business measurement standard.

Our economy is complex, so there is no single problem to fix. There are many problems. However, we can link our most serious social, environmental, economic and business problems to one major underlying problem. From it, stem further complications. So, while it won't solve all problems, it influences many. If we only address a single problem, this should be it. It will make a huge difference in providing balance to our economy.

The problem I am referring to is our inadequate and inappropriate business measurement standard. It focuses business, through every action and process, to create a profit for its shareholders (owners of the business,) without regard to the interests of other constituents or stakeholders (other entities involved in the business - staff, environment, etc.) This is not surprising as it's a financial measurement standard. However, financial measures account for less than twenty per cent of business value. That should give you a hint as to why it's an inadequate and inappropriate business measurement standard. Finance is not business - it's only a small part of business.

So, despite knowing its inadequate and inappropriate as a business measurement standard, why do we persist in using it? Because it serves shareholder needs. Their first priority is to optimise profits, which they achieve by using an inadequate and inappropriate measurement standard, which serves their needs only.

No doubt you've heard Capitalism blamed for our economic problems, but have you ever heard of our inadequate and inappropriate business measurement standard blamed? Of course not because that's what they want hidden. They will do everything to create smokescreens, mislead and draw your attention away from it because when you know what's the major cause of our problems, you will demand change. You will demand we introduce a new, balanced and fair standard (which looks after the needs of all stakeholders.) However, introducing a new, balanced and fair standard will severely curtail their wealth creation potential. Naturally, they will do everything to stop this from happening.

This chapter highlights how bad our business measurement standard is, and how it has turned us into nothing more than the worst form of profiteers. It also explains that a new, balanced measurement framework is available - that it's not elusive, as they would have us believe.

We should all get behind the call to replace our inadequate and inappropriate business measurement standard as it will play the biggest role in restoring economic balance. Under no circumstances must you confuse this imperative with CSR (Corporate Social Responsibility) or IR (Integrated Reporting) initiatives, which in no way address our measurement needs. We need a radical, new approach to business measurement. It involves more than cobbling together disparate reports onto financial reports, as the two aforementioned "solutions" suggest.

Chapter 2
Stop and redress free market growth.

Vested interest's first priority is to maximise profits by using an inadequate and inappropriate measurement standard which looks after their needs exclusively. Their second priority is to increase profits by removing restrictions applied by governments to protect (often vulnerable) interests. These "free markets", free from government intervention, lead directly to increased wealth for them.

Vested interests claim that removing government interference (or regulations) will mean markets run more efficiently and as a consequence, their increased profits benefit all. Their wealth "trickles down" to benefit everybody. This is a fallacy - very little "trickles down." First, how can a system set up to exclusively serve shareholder needs be considered to be efficient? It represents the misuse of resources - using resources only for the benefit of shareholders. Therefore, removing regulations will allow for greater misuse of resources. Rather than reduce government involvement, which is what "free markets" require, we need greater government involvement and business regulation, to protect vulnerable stakeholders from business's profiteering practices.

Globalisation and free markets are not the same things. Globalisation is about access to global markets. However access to these markets works better for business when there are fewer restrictions, or regulations, (i.e. "free markets.") This is what vested interests want and that's what they've made globalisation all about - global free markets. So, globalisation represents free market thinking applied to international markets. The aim of free markets and globalisation is to establish an economic order which transcends the power of national states. They want to remove the influence and control of nation-states, thereby providing them "free" or open global markets. This means they can produce anywhere (globally, wherever it's cheap) and sell everywhere, with no restrictions/interventions. This is highly beneficial for them, but not for you or I.

These transnationals have no concerns for the well-being of the citizens of nation-states, who lose their jobs and suffer the consequences, as manufacturing moves from their country to low labour cost countries. They're only concerned with optimising their profits. Business works on the principle of the "survival of the fittest." Government's, on the other hand, concern themselves with the well-being of all their citizens, particularly the weak and vulnerable. To this end, they implement laws and regulations to protect and nurture their citizens, as well as protect their natural resources. Vested interests want these laws and regulations discarded so they can exploit these resources, to increase their wealth.

Unless business self-regulates more effectively through a new, balanced measurement standard, governments must step in and protect the vulnerable. Allowing business a free-hand without improved self-regulation guarantees the spread of economic enslavement. Scaling this problem up to a global level magnifies the problem, weakening nation-states so they can no longer effectively serve their citizen's needs. We see this problem in all developed economies today.

Free markets and globalisation are a nation's worst enemy. We must not only stop its advance but actively reintroduce laws and regulations to start protecting citizens of these nation-states. Governments need to start rebuilding the quality-of-life for their citizens by taking back control and becoming more involved in economic affairs, not less involved.

Chapter 3
Stop and redress rentier economy growth.

What we've learnt so far is that business uses a measurement standard to optimises shareholder wealth, at the expense of all others. They then strip away protective laws and regulations so they can generate even more profit from so called "free markets." Again, this is done at the expense of all others. Free markets also weaken the economic negotiating strength of nations, which allows vested interests to hold governments over a barrel, thereby increasing their wealth further. So, what's driving economic inequality should now be evident.

The wealth they create does not "trickle down" to benefit all as claimed. In fact, it's used to leverage even more wealth. Consequently, economic inequality grows rapidly. The two aforementioned factors are by no means the only contributors to inequality, but are significant. Most of the wealth held by the one per cent is not reinvested in our "active" economy but redirected out into the "rentier" economy, to the detriment of our "active" economy and most of us. Investing in the "rentier" economy benefits them, and harms us. So, making the wealthy richer hurts the average citizen - it does not help them.

Trickle down is a hoax. The wealthy one per cent know it doesn't work. They hide their true intentions behind it. They know by increasing inequality, this creates economic scarcity in the middle/low-income groups, which leads to insecurity and instability. The wealthy then create systems and practices to prey on these people's vulnerabilities. Credit abuse and gambling are just two examples. This is called the "Vacuum Up" effect, and in contrast to trickle down, it works extremely well. It allows the wealthy to vacuum up every morsel of wealth from the poor classes. It adds significantly to the wealthy one per cents wealth.

In this chapter, I will elaborate on the economic and social problems caused by economic inequality and the problems the rentier economy creates. It is highly likely that because of entrenched systems, practices and procedures now in place, we face the prospect of ever-increasing economic inequality. This will take us back in time, away from hard-earned equality, to an era of "lord and master." However, in today's society, it will be increasingly difficult to hide such gross inequality. It's a potential social time-bomb. Economic hardship drives social hardship, which could quite easily blow up in the face of the rich. There is no justification for the continued existence of these unfair economic practices. It is economic apartheid and it must go.

If you are unclear about terms like "active" and "rentier" economy, or any other terms or arguments used so far, please don't worry, I will explain them in more detail in their relevant chapter.

Chapter 4
Create a true investment culture.

You have learnt how the rich have used an inadequate and inappropriate measurement standard to optimise profits for themselves. How they then manipulate the markets to ensure they are free from regulations, so they can generate even greater profits. How their wealth does not trickle down as the hoax proclaimed it would. Instead, it's used to leverage further wealth opportunities, using the vacuum up effect, and to invest in the rentier economy. This increases their wealth even further. However, there remains one other major opportunity for them to exploit, and that's the investment market.

Investment is an important contributor to economic growth. Therefore, you would assume we have a solid and sensible investment culture to support our economy. Unfortunately, that's not what we have. Instead, vested interests have hijacked the field of investment to serve their needs, not ours. We have lost all sight of the basics of investment and adopted a short-term commodity trading mentality. Shares have become nothing more than commodities, traded as often as they can for profit. These changes don't serve our needs.

Vested interests have changed how our investment community operates and shifted the emphasis onto commodity trading based on limited short-term market information ("blips.") Short-term market "blips" in the form of trading data, quarterly, half-yearly and annual results, as well as rumours and other minor market events, cause market fluctuations, against which they trade shares. Short-term, insignificant market "blips", drive markets. These "blips" (generally) do not impact on true investors. True investors concern themselves with achieving long-term objectives and persevere, despite short-term setbacks.

This shift in emphasis has meant we don't have long-term owners of businesses, but rather short-term share certificate owners. These share certificate owners aren't concerned in the long-term growth of the business, only in it is short-term share price and dividends, as they can divest themselves of their "investment" in less than minutes. These shareholders shift their responsibilities onto "proxy owners" - professional managers, whose job is to serve their share certificate holders. In other words, they aren't interested in long-term results either, only what satisfies their paymaster. As short-term profits and dividends are their objectives, this sets off a series of activities which denude business's of value, but adds to short-term profit and dividends. However, these activities leave businesses weaker, and their survival over the long-term becomes problematic. This does not serve the wider community's needs.

We have to return to the basics of investment to stabilise markets and give the economy real growth opportunities, which will benefit all. Again, this is a case of vested interests manipulating practices, procedures and systems to serve their needs, not those of the wider community. It is a significant contributor towards economic injustice.

Chapter 5
Rein in rampant consumerism - act collectively.
Economic injustice is obviously of paramount importance, but it's a secondary concern when compared to ensuring we have a healthy and supportive environment in which to live. The stark reality is - we cannot sustain current levels of consumption, waste, pollution and environmental degradation and achieve this. We face population growth and emerging economies who expect to live like their counterparts in developed economies. This is a disaster waiting to happen, and it's just around the corner.

Our economic systems, practices and procedures, together with the misleading perceptions fed the majority, underlie these environmental problems. It's all part of the same economic screw-up and it's driven by the wealthy one per cent's greed and self-interest. They drive rampant consumption as it adds to their wealth. However, they don't concern themselves with its consequences, as that lies within the domain of "the common good." This does not concern them. Their only concern is to make a profit, and not to be "caught with blood on their hands" (i.e. not to be found responsible for any adverse environmental/social consequences.) To ensure we continue consuming like there's no tomorrow, they concoct messages and promote them to change our perceptions. They encourage consumption, telling us not to worry about the consequences, as they are taken care of. They relentlessly feed society with these messages and cover up the consequences as best they can, until the person-in-the-street believes it as the truth.

Consequently, we live in a society where we, as consumers, believe we can consume as we please, with little or no regard to the effects. The reality is entirely different. The planet cannot sustain current levels of consumption, with all its negative consequences, let alone grow. As consumers, we need to accept greater responsibility for our consumption, despite what vested interests tell us. The message we have been fed for decades is that we have "earned the right to consume" as we work hard, and not to worry about the consequences as that's taken care of. Nobody "earns the right" to destroy our environment, as we only have temporary use of it. Besides, everyone knows we have not taken care of the consequences, such as sustainability, waste, pollution and environmental degradation. However, it's been easy and convenient for us to believe the lies we have been fed, although now the stark realities are starting to sink in. We too, have to accept responsibility for our actions. It's not only a problem created by vested interests. We establish the demand which business tries to fulfil. Therefore, we need to temper our demands based on reality.

Accordingly, we need to introduce changes which hold businesses responsible and accountable for driving rampant consumerism. Changing our business measurement standard will achieve this. However, we as consumers have been far too complacent in accepting vested interests insidious messages about our right to consume wantonly, with no regard for the consequences. Therefore, we cannot solve the problems by censuring business alone as the consumer is a vital link in the supply chain. We need to review the social contract between business and consumer, to make consumers more responsible. "Inclusive Theory" provides the framework for this new contract. It sees the problem holistically and suggests we find the solution by working together in accepting responsibility. We cannot hold business responsible if consumers do not accept their share of responsibility. I explain what Inclusive Theory entails in this chapter.

The collapse of planetary resources under the pressure of greater demand is not solely a sustainability problem, as you will appreciate, but also a massive socioeconomic problem, which needs to be high on our agenda.

Chapter 6
Increase government involvement.

The next five chapters, including this, address what's needed to reverse the rapid decline in the quality-of-life of the middle/low-income groups - ninety-nine per cent of the population. Over the past four decades, there has been a relentless process afoot, of taking from the poor and giving to the rich - the Dooh Nibor process. The Robin Hood story in reverse; manipulated and controlled by the wealthy one per cent.

Government is responsible for its citizen's well-being. It has to put an end to apartheid economics - economic injustice imposed upon the majority. This requires big government to evaluate, implement and enforce what's in the interest of the majority. Small government cannot do it. They do not have the necessary resources. Government has to take the lead in addressing the four key inequality drivers mentioned in chapters one to four. They also have to take the lead in addressing rampant consumerism, and environmental issues as elaborated in Chapter Five. The other chapters in this book also need significant government involvement. This involves a lot of resources - it requires BIG GOVERNMENTS.

The wealthy one per cent don't want big governments. They will tell you its inefficient and a waste of taxpayers money. This is just another of their lies to hide the real reasons. Big governments bring the perspective of "what's best for the majority", rather than allow business a free hand in doing what they want to optimise profits. Vested interests don't want this intervention; they want what's best for them. A government with little resource cannot ensure the interests of the majority is served, and this gives them the opportunity to profit unfairly.

As an example of this, a small government is less effective in collecting tax (as they don't have the resources to do so.) This results in increased tax avoidance and evasion. Smaller governments are more vulnerable to economic threats as they don't have the resources to evaluate them effectively and therefore succumb to them. This means small governments have regressive tax regimes, where the wealthy pay less pro rata tax than the poor. That's the purpose of free markets and globalisation to reduce the size of government and weaken them. In this way, they can hold governments to ransom by threatening to relocate their business elsewhere, or reduce investment if governments don't meet their demands.

So, increasing government size is important in keeping vested interests in check, but government involvement must go much further. They should play a greater role in providing services and support for business, to ensure a thriving and prosperous economy. However, government's role extends far beyond economics. They are responsible for ensuring a high quality-of-life for all. How can we achieve this if governments do not become deeply involved in the many services needed to accomplish this? If high quality-of-life is the objective (which it is), then big government is a necessity.

Of course, vested interests don't want big governments because they are costly and its funding will fall on those who can afford it, namely, the wealthy and corporates. This will reduce their wealth; something they vehemently oppose. So, they promote misleading information to protect their wealth, as the well-being of a nation's citizens is not their concern, only protecting their wealth. They claim big government leads to a socialist state of lazy people. However, the opposite is true. Society's attitude towards risk changes and innovation improves when government provides good safety nets and support. This leads to greater productivity and competitiveness, thereby expanding the economy. Lowering people's quality-of-life produces the complete opposite. Small government's lower citizens quality-of-life, as they provide citizens with fewer services and support. Providing a high quality-of-life is what good governance is all about, and that involves big governments.

Chapter 7
Make small business development a priority.

We have to see the importance of small business development in the same light as we view education and training. Both play a critical role in broadening our economic base and thus the standard-of-living and quality-of-life for all. Business, just like us, goes through a life cycle. We have to ensure we have a robust, healthy and well-prepared crop of new businesses starting out every year; otherwise, the future won't be bright. This requires a highly supportive government. It's not just about skills and knowledge, but about a supportive society and business environment. This requires big governments and a long-term vision and commitment to small business development.

However, vested interests don't want this (despite paying lip service to the idea.) Firstly, they oppose the idea of big government, as it "hinders" their wealth creation abilities and reduces their wealth (through higher taxes.) Equally importantly, they don't want future competitors or disrupters entering their markets. Because of these concerns, they make sure governments don't commit to this important facet of our economic development, which must change so we may all benefit. Again, this is another facet of economic life manipulated by vested interests, in fostering their needs over those of the wider community.

Chapter 8
Stop chasing unmanaged growth.

Most politicians and therefore governments, have this unfounded belief that the economy must grow every year because that's what's good for us. Nothing can be further from the truth. It's based on a misunderstanding that if there's more money coming in because of growth, then we must be better off. Unfortunately, that's not true. Growth per se is no guarantee of being better off. It all depends upon one's underlying financials. If these financials are right (or managed correctly), then growth benefits most, but if they're wrong, it hurts most. So, we need to manage our underlying financials to ensure beneficial growth. Governments are ignoring these fundamentals because they are under pressure from the wealthy one per cent to do so.

Governments who chase unmanaged GDP growth are similar to businesses who pursue sales growth without due consideration for their underlying financials and fall into the trap of "overtrading." It's a serious problem which leads to the collapse of business and lower quality-of-life for a government's citizens. So, to believe growth under any circumstances is good, is a reckless and harmful policy to follow, but it's a policy which benefits vested interests.

Over the past two decades, the UK has seen GDP growth. However, its underlying financials have been poor. It's been unable to support growth. In other words, it has "overtraded", which has meant the consistent lowering of citizen's quality-of-life, year-on-year. Growth has hurt, not helped us. Unless we address the underlying financials, growth will continue to hurt, not help. The UK reflects the situation across most developed economies.

So why should governments get themselves into this unenviable position? Vested interests force governments into unmanaged growth for three reasons.

- Growth serves their short-term profit needs. They are the ones who create the hype and put pressure on governments to grow GDP continually, to serve their needs, irrespective of the hardship it may cause others. However, they would never knowingly "overtrade" themselves.

- Governments are "punished" globally if they don't grow GDP, as GDP is a macroeconomic measure which serves the wealthy one per cent. It's another inadequate and inappropriate measure.

- The wealthy one per cent are the major contributors to factors which make it difficult for governments to address their underlying financials effectively.

The secret to controlling outcomes is to create measures which give you the results you want. We see this at a microeconomic level through our business measurement standard and at a macroeconomic level through measuring GDP. Both are inadequate and inappropriate but they serve the needs of the wealthy one per cent, so that's why we keep them. However, we can't continue like this. The solution requires political will to address underlying financial problems and to implement major change to our economic systems, particularly our measures.

Chapter 9
Encourage manufacturing.

We are a society of consumers, and this will not change. However, we need to produce what we consume. The less a country produces, the more it has to import; the worse its balance of payments. In the long-term, the country becomes a net consumer, not a producer. To fund this, it has to borrow instead of having a surplus to invest. The more manufacturing the government allows to leave its shores the more vulnerable the economy becomes in the long-term as services are not a good substitute (despite what vested interests tell us.)

Globalisation and free markets are the cause of this loss in manufacturing, and it's harmful to national economies who lose their manufacturing to low labour cost countries. Vested interests have no concern for the well-being of citizens who lose their jobs and national economies impacted through these losses. They only concern themselves with their own profits and well-being.

Protectionism is only a dirty word in the vocabulary of Big Business as it limits market access and profits. It should be a word welcomed and implemented (prudently) by governments and their citizens. Governments must protect their industries in their long-term interests, particularly strategically important industries. Vested interests promote ideas like globalisation, free markets and anti-protectionism solely for their benefit. These ideas don't help the majority. Sadly, political perceptions are manipulated, which sees politicians beating vested interest's drum, ignorant of the harm they are inflicting on their constituents.

What's more, moving goods globally ignores, or pays little attention to environmental and sustainability issues. Environmental costs are not correctly accounted for and sustainability issues overlooked. In the future, we will come to appreciate fully that environmental costs are prohibitively high, and unsustainable, making local production essential. AI

(Artificial Intelligence) and robotics will soon negate low labour cost countries advantage, making local production price competitive. So we don't want to lose our manufacturing base for short-term gains which only benefit a few.

Chapter 10
Realign our higher education system.

We are not producing the knowledge and skills business needs, and neither are we investing enough in higher education and training. This results in many problems, principally, a poorly performing economy, which impacts on all. Business must accept full responsibility for this. Their obsession with short-term profit has seen them relinquish control over the education and training process, despite paying lip service to its importance.

As business has not accepted financial responsibility (supported by the government), others have taken control over the process, resulting in a disconnect of the parties concerned; all pulling in different directions. We are employed to carry out work. The more effective our training and education to undertake this work, the happier and more productive we should be. The best place for this training to take place is at work. Places of work need to become places of learning, supported by educational institutions. Higher education institutions, such as universities, should not be places of education, but for research.

Only through a change in our measurement standard, which fully recognises the need for training and education, can fundamental change to our higher education system take place. Our current measurement standard discourages this investment. Businesses, assisted by the government, need to manage and fund education and training more effectively, to meet their needs. In this way, businesses will become places of learning, supported by educational institutions. As a result, the economy will grow and with it the standard-of-living and quality-of-life for all.

I talk a lot about economic inequality, but there is a facet we must not lose sight of, and that is opportunity inequality. It's directly linked to economic inequality. As economic inequality worsens so to does opportunity inequality. Opportunities for the majority get smaller and smaller while those for the rich get bigger and better. With the proposed changes, to our higher education system, fairer access to higher education should become more achievable - leading to greater opportunity for most.

The ideas recommended in this chapter are predicated upon government ensuring a higher primary education standard. This involves wider social support, making sure citizens have access to housing, health and other welfare support. Education does not function in a vacuum. It functions best in a highly supportive environment. We achieve success through cooperation, and that requires a supportive social environment.

Chapter 11
New epoch - new rules.

Every day we hear or read about AI (Artificial Intelligence), robotics, and conscious computers. People have different opinions on whether these new technologies will benefit or destroy us. However, one thing is for sure; they herald a new epoch for man. This is not a revolution but an epoch. An epoch represents an age, and during an age, a few revolutions may occur. An epoch is something far bigger than a revolution.

Therefore, there is no question about it; we are about to face massive change. Whether this will benefit or destroy us depends upon what economic environment it's introduced into. I think the introduction of these new technologies will have dire consequences if introduced into our current self-serving economy, geared to serve a few, with little or no concern for the common good. Therefore, if we are to minimise the effects this new epoch will have on labour, we need a new set of rules, and we need them fast. We need wide changing economic reform, but most importantly we need a new measurement standard which considers the wider good, not just the interests of shareholders. We also need large government to consider the broader picture and implement what's best for the majority. Small government can't do that. Under a new regime, this new epoch should be hugely beneficial.

If you think this new epoch will not affect you because of the job you do - think again. It will place every job at risk. If you want to protect yourself and your family from vested interests who put their interests before anything else, then support changes to our economic systems now.

How to become involved.

Throughout this introduction, I have made reference to how the wealthy one per cent have, over the past forty years, influenced every facet of society. They have done so through a continuous stream of disinformation, falsehoods, half-truths and obfuscation. Through the manipulation and coercion of government, regulatory bodies, professional institutions and virtually all entities who can serve or hinder their wealth creation objectives. They have changed perceptions to the extent that people quote and believe the nonsense fed them without question as if they are some immutable laws of the universe. In reality, as this book will show, they are nothing of the sort. They are there for no other reason than to enrich a few. These ingrained beliefs, supported by unjust systems and backed by powerful, influential and determined people, is what we need to overturn.

The only way to bring about much-needed change is through mobilising mass demand, calling on governments to support and implement change. In a democracy, we have the power to change things, but only if we act collectively - we represent ninety-nine per cent of the population. As an individual, it's like standing in front of a well-defended fortress armed with a peashooter. If you don't think the issues raised in this book will affect you or your family, I strongly suggest you reconsider. Every issue affects you or your family, either directly or indirectly - and you can change them.

Please read the book. Identify areas of interest. Understand the problems and solutions so you can express yourself clearly. If unclear on any issue, please write to me, I'm more than happy to help. Get your network of colleagues, friends and family involved and spread the news among them. Encourage them to spread the news. Encourage them to keep up the pressure. Write to, and visit your local MP. Ensure they have a copy of this book. Ask them to raise the problem in parliament. Contact local news media, ask them what they are doing to spread the news and what they are doing in calling for change. Join the debate as we need to spread the message far and wide, and we need to do it now. We also need to keep the pressure up. It's your, and your family's future at stake - please spread the word!

Thank you,
Adrian Dore,
Bristol,
United Kingdom.

Chapter 1
Replace our inadequate and inappropriate business measurement standard.

Public opinion believes our economy no longer serves the needs of the many -
What A Screw-Up!

Why is this? What's the cause?
There are many causes, but let's start by identifying the single biggest cause by far.

To do that let's look in the most obvious place of all - our business measurement standard. It's the obvious place to look because businesses form the micro building blocks of our economy, and what we measure is what we get. If we set up our measurement standard to serve the needs of a particular group, excluding all others - surprise, surprise, that's the result we get.

By serving the needs of an exclusive group, excluding all others, business produces imbalanced outcomes. This lies at the heart of our problem (and therefore, by extension our economy.) In less than a minute, we have been able to identify the source of our problem. If the source is easily identified; in plain sight for all to see why is it never mentioned as the root cause of our problems?

Simple - it serves the needs of a small, elite, influential group of vested interests. It's their primary tool for optimising profits. They want it protected (at all costs.) They don't want it replaced by a fairer, balanced standard, which would serve the needs of all stakeholders. They want business to work for them alone, so our business measures focus on the outcomes they want and expect.

The problem is, how do they hide the biggest cause of our economic screw-up, which is in plain sight, and easily identified? If the public knew the facts, they would demand its immediate replacement.

Build a smokescreen.

The best strategy to follow is to blame something else and create a big enough hype around this accusation to build a smokescreen which hides the real cause. These are powerful and influential people, more than capable of doing this. And, that's precisely what they've done.

The ideal candidate to blame is Capitalism, as it's a concept vaguely understood by the populace, and considered by many to favour greedy fat cats, at everybody else's expense. This fits the bill perfectly. So, they promote the idea we operate under a Capitalist system - that we are Capitalists. The man in the street knows there's something wrong with our economy, and they see these "greedy fat cat Capitalists" everywhere. They feel the economic pinch and see the environmental damage done by these "fat cats" all around them. The next step is easy - they blame Capitalism. "Capitalism is the cause our problems", nothing else can be to blame. Now, all vested interests have to do is keep the fires of this lie well stoked, and we will continue to chase our tails.

To ensure these fires remain well stoked, vested interests create and actively back organisations that blame Capitalism for our economic woes. They also create and back organisations whose supposed purpose is to help Capitalism become "more inclusive," to include, somehow, the many millions marginalised by our economic system. By creating and supporting both antagonist and protagonist, they keep the fires burning bright, diverting attention as far away from the real cause as possible.

Through these and other efforts, Capitalism, as our supposed "problem", remains high on the public agenda, yet our inadequate and inappropriate measurement standard, the real cause, is unheard of. Have you ever heard it mentioned as the cause of our problems.? No - never. I must admit, they have done a brilliant job in diverting attention away from the real cause. It's never mentioned as the root cause of our most serious social, environmental, economic and business problems, despite this being true. Their manipulation is awe-inspiring. However, there are a few rumblings within the business community, as many businesses bear the brunt of this inadequate and inappropriate measurement standard. Vested interests deal with these murmurings in a different, but equally deceptive way. I will explain these deceptions later in the chapter.

Continuing to confuse and mislead us.

Their manipulation doesn't stop here, it's pervasive in every respect. As an example of one of their more subtle manipulations, they have conflated the terms "standard-of-living" and "quality-of-life." This may not appear to be important, or relevant, and yet it is critically so. These are two distinct terms defining entirely different things. They are both important measures in gauging our well-being. There is no question, we have a rising standard-of-living, but our quality-of-life is in rapid decline, and it's our quality-of-life, which influences our well-being the most. (For more details, please refer to Appendix A.)

There's a good reason they have conflated these terms. When challenged about our rapidly declining quality-of-life, they respond by pointing to our rising standard-of-living, saying, "What's the problem, things are on the up and up." The conflation enables them to hide that rather than doing well, we are, in fact, doing badly. They don't want you and I to know how badly our economic systems are serving us. They need to present a positive picture, to mask the unpleasant and harsh realities the average citizen faces. They need to confuse and mislead us. We will introduce further falsehoods, bad practices and systems throughout this book. All the things implemented to serve their needs, irrespective of the depths they plum in achieving them. These are all the things we need to change.

Capitalism is not the problem.

Now you know Capitalism is only a smokescreen. We investigate Capitalism in more depth, so you can see, beyond any question or doubt, it's not the culprit. That it's used to hide the real cause of our problems.

First, Capitalism is an ideology. It's a set of ideals and beliefs. It's not a system, practice, or procedure by which we run and manage business. It's these systems, practices and procedures which we use every day to run and manage business which produce the outcomes which cause our problems. We use the Accounting Model, a financial measurement standard, to run and manage business. This causes our problems as it emphasises financial considerations, ignoring other critical business success factors. This is understandable as it's only a financial measure. However, financial measures only account for less than twenty per cent of the value creation potential of business, yet despite this, it's used as our business performance measure. Obviously, in this role, it's entirely inadequate and inappropriate, as it ignores the impact of other stakeholders, who contribute over eighty per cent of the wealth/value creation potential of business.

Second, as an ideology, its aim is not to create profits. Profit creation is an essential component of Capitalism, as it's a means to an end, but it's not its objective. This is in stark contrast to that of our inadequate and inappropriate measurement standard (our Accounting Model), whose sole aim is short-term profit creation to benefit shareholders.

The purpose or objective of Capitalism is "to serve the needs of humanity in a sustainable manner through the ingenuity of man, allowed to engage in free enterprise." The operative words are "sustainable manner." This requires a balanced approach in meeting the needs of all business participants (or stakeholders.) An imbalanced system, serving only the needs of one or more participant cannot survive over the long-term and falls short of the fundamental requirement of serving all. While profit is an essential component of Capitalism, clearly it isn't its objective. Business needs to make a profit to survive, so profit is a means to an end, not the end in itself. If profit were its aim, it would not survive or meet its real objectives. Our profit obsession (as dictated by our Accounting Model) is the antithesis of Capitalism.

Third, by blaming Capitalism, an ideology, it's difficult to pin specifics on it. Whereas, with our measurement standard (the real cause of our problems,) we can link it directly to our most serious social, environmental, economic and business problems. So, by blaming Capitalism people cannot come up with specific problems and therefore, specific solutions. As a result, they go around in circles chasing their tails. This is precisely what vested interests want.

Capitalism is a practical ideology.
Free-enterprise (not "free markets" - which is something entirely different) lies at the heart of Capitalism. Free-enterprise is good, as it encourages ingenuity and hard work. This, leads to a continuous improvement in our standard-of-living, which is an important consideration.

The simple definition of Capitalism (as stated earlier,) shows it in no way represents the economic system we now follow. "The objective of Capitalism is to serve the needs of humanity in a sustainable manner through the ingenuity of man, allowed to engage in free-enterprise." What's not to like about this ideology? To serve the needs of humanity, business must make a profit to survive over the long-term. Profit making is essential, but we have corrupted it and made it our purpose. This is not Capitalism - this is the result of a short-term financial measurement standard dictating business outcomes.

If we replace our inadequate and inappropriate business measurement standard with a balanced standard, looking after the needs of all participants, then we can uphold the objectives of Capitalism. We have to see profit as a means to an end, and not the end in itself. Until then, we are definitely not Capitalists.

We aren't what we call ourselves.
We can call ourselves Capitalists if we want, but that does not make us what we say we are if we don't follow its ideology. Just as we may call ourself a Christian or Jew (or any other faith,) that does not make us what we say we are unless we follow the philosophy of what we claim to be.

What we are is what we do every day in our life. The same applies to business. What it does every day represents what our economy really is, because, business is at the heart of our economy.

We call ourselves Capitalists because we follow the principles of free enterprise, but this is not enough to qualify us as Capitalists. We don't serve the long-term interests of humanity – we serve the interests of a few. We are not Capitalists, but something far more sinister. We are what we do every day in business. Our business measurement standard dictates what we do every day in business as measures dictate outcomes. These outcomes represent the ideology we follow. They show us who we are by reflecting what we do every day, not what we say we are.

What are we if not Capitalists?
We use a financial measure as our business measurement standard, despite financial considerations accounting for less than twenty per cent of the wealth/value creation potential of business. Its aim is to optimise short-term profit exclusively for the benefit of shareholders, at the expense of other stakeholders (or participants.) It's an adversarial system which is pitted against the interest's of stakeholders, only considering shareholder interests.

By definition, this makes it a profiteering system. We define a profiteering system as one which uses an unfair advantage to generate a profit. The "unfair advantage" here is a measurement standard which does not consider the interests of other stakeholders. It only gives weight and credence to financial matters without due considerations to other interrelated participant needs.

We usually associate profiteering as an external activity where business profits from an external entity like a customer, competitor, or government, using some unfair advantage. However, in this case it's the worst form of profiteering as it's "internal profiteering." This is the worst form of profiteering because shareholders profit from those associated with them in trying to make them more prosperous.

So, we are not Capitalists but profiteers - the worst form of profiteers, those who exploit their own stakeholders for profit. Understandably vested interests want this kept from public knowledge because armed with this understanding, are you prepared to allow this harmful practice to continue?

Who knows of the problem?

I don't believe most business people, including accountants, and those in senior positions, understand the full extent of the harm caused by using our inadequate and inappropriate business measurement standard. They acknowledge "it's not perfect," but tell you "it's the language of business." This indicates they have accepted it and believe it can't be changed. This is what they are told and believe. They are only the "troops" who follow through on well-practised drills. They don't question them - that's the role of the generals, to create the strategy and rules of engagement. Generals don't publicise their strategy. They formulate plans which only a small group of staff officers - the inner circle, know about.

Just as politicians and our democratic processes are influenced by wealth, so too are business's regulatory bodies and institutions. The inner circle of these regulatory bodies and institutions which decide on policy and strategy dance to the tune of the wealthy one per cent. They implement what serves the one per cent's needs, and they know precisely what's going on. They are the ones who implement their organisation's strategies to confuse and mislead us. They (through their influence) put in place laws, policies, practices and procedures to serve their master's interests. They are no more than puppets, which manoeuvre the pieces on the chessboard to ensure they achieve their objectives of increasing and protecting their master's interests, irrespective of the cost to others.

Accountants are the profession at the centre of this problem. It's their Accounting Model, used inappropriately as a business measure, which is the root cause of our most serious problems. However, as I've already said, I don't think the average accountant fully knows the full extent of the problem. They know that their measures are inadequate as a business measure but not much more. Way back in 1987, members of their own fraternity published a book written about the inadequacies of their Accounting Model as a business measure.

So accountants generally appreciate there's a problem, but not the full extent, as you now understand it, having read this book so far. Their own profession misleads them into not seeing the problem's full extent. They have hidden the amplitude of it, despite it being so obvious and something they work with daily.

A pretence at finding a solution.

Because, the accounting profession, and other business professions know of the inadequacies of the Accounting Model, those who represent the profession make a pretence of doing something about it. However, accounting institutes and their masters don't want change, particularly seismic change which will see accountants lose their dominant role, and with it their income and influence. Shareholders and investors will have their profits slashed. Therefore, preserving the Accounting Model as our business measurement standard is critical to them and the wealthy one **per cent**. They don't want it changed under any circumstance. So, rather than address the problem, they implement a PR campaign which has them looking busy, while doing nothing. I will present you the facts, and you be the judge on whether you think they are serious in addressing the problem.

If you know what the problem is, then you should have a fairly good idea of what the requirements are for a solution, particularly if you are close to the problem, working with it daily. However, over the past thirty years, despite knowing of the problems and having a good idea of what a solution should look like, they have come up with nothing. These are bright, capable people, with enormous resources at their disposal, so this alone should be evidence enough that their heart and soul is not in any effort to find a solution. They aren't investing in a problem-solving exercise, but in a PR campaign to mislead us into thinking they are doing something about it.

Let's look at what our requirements for a solution should be; then we will compare them with what the accounting profession is proposing as a "solution". You then determine for yourself if they are genuinely committed to finding a solution, or undertaking nothing more than a PR campaign, making sure nothing changes, but seen as being "busy trying."

Determining our requirements.

We base our broad requirements for a new measurement standard on some fundamental understanding of business, such as:-

1. Business functions as a cause-and-effect (or causal) model.
2. A causal model is fully inclusive of all constituents (or parts,) based on their interrelationships.
3. Value creation is the common denominator of business (i.e. it is the common objective of all business processes.)
4. Therefore, by inference, business is based on a value creation causal model.
5. We need a clear understanding of this model; it's structures and interrelationships, to be able to measure and manage business effectively, to optimise value creation opportunities for all constituents or stakeholders.

A new measurement standard must meet these specific requirements. It must be:-

1. **Comparable:** Our economy relies on comparable measures across all businesses irrespective of sector or size. Incomparable measures are valueless to the market (i.e. investors.)

2. **Relevant:** It has to solve our need - to provide insight into the value creation potential of business for all stakeholders, including shareholders.

3. **Reliable:** Our new measurement standard needs to be prescriptive. It needs to be specific on what to measure and how to measure. It needs to establish the rules and standards and they need to be assured.

4. **Simple/easily understandable:** It has to apply to all. It cannot just apply to large business. Every business irrespective of sector or size must be able to use it as they use the Accounting Model. Therefore, it has to be simple and easy to understand.

5. **Useful:** It has to provide a road map which even the smallest business can understand and use to help unlock value creation for all constituents, or stakeholders.

Let's now have a look at the major "solutions" proposed by the accounting fraternity (comprising their institutes, associations, academics and leading practitioners) to see how they match our requirements.

There are only two fundamental questions we need to ask to see if a proposal has any chance of providing a solution in becoming our new measurement standard. I call these our "two minimum requirements." The first is, "Is the solution based on any understanding of the value creation causal model?" This is the underlying model all business operate on, so it's rather important we base our measures on this model. Second, "Is the solution comparable across all business sectors, irrespective of sector or size?" Also, an important consideration, because our economy relies on the need to compare to invest. Non-comparable measures are valueless.

The "solutions" we will look at are as follows:-
1. Global Reporting Initiative.
2. IIRC (International Integrated Reporting Council.)
3. UN Reporting Framework.
4. Ernst & Young LTV (Long Term Value model.)

None of these "solutions" are based on any understanding of the underlying mechanics of business - the value creation causal model. None of the solutions provide any comparable measures. So, they don't come remotely close to meeting our "two minimum requirements." Although this list is not extensive, none of the other less well known "solutions" fare any better.

I have not included CSR (Corporate Social Responsibility) reporting as it's a concept that's been with us for over two decades and has had little or no impact. These reports have proved to be nothing more than PR opportunities for Big Business (Volkswagen emissions scandal being a case in point.) These are addenda to financial reports and as such miss the point of the need to see business holistically. To base our measurement and reporting on an understanding of the value creation causal model, which is an integrated and interrelated model. CSR reports have no understanding of how the components of business are integrated and interrelated. Therefore, how can they add value? All they are doing is cobbling together disparate reports, which confuse rather than provide clarity.

If the accounting fraternity were genuine in finding a solution, then at least, with all the resources at their disposal, they should have been able to identify our "two minimum requirements." What's there to challenge in the logic used in arriving at these requirements? The simple truth is - they don't want a solution and aren't looking for one.

A workable solution is available.

Over twenty years ago I became involved in trying to find out how business goes about creating value for all its constituents (or stakeholders.) I recognised the importance of understanding the underlying mechanics of business - the value creation causal model and the importance of providing comparable measures. Over this time I worked on finding a workable solution. One which I know is capable of meeting all our requirements, despite what others may say that business does not share enough in common to support a common value creation measurement framework - NONSENSE!. What do they know? They haven't done any work to find out. They are too busy trying not to solve the problem.

I have challenged many in the accounting fraternity to explain why they talk so glibly about value creation but have no understanding of the underlying mechanism for creating it. They don't want to talk to people like myself, who have an understanding of the value creation causal model, because such an understanding threatens their dominant position. I'm a disruptive influence who will see financial accounting relegated to a small part of overall business management. Financial management accounts for less than twenty per cent of business's value creation potential. Accountants don't want change, and neither do the wealthy one per cent, as it serves their needs perfectly.

It is our understanding of the value creation causal model which will provide us with a fully inclusive measurement standard, managing the value creation needs of all business constituents (or stakeholders.) This will place business on an even keel, serving the needs of all stakeholders, thus fulfilling its role as a valuable social tool.

Environmental and social concerns.

There is no way to deny or escape the reality - we are in the process of irreparably damaging the planet and its ecology. We are destroying what sustains us. We have to stop what we are doing and change our ways, and we have to do it now. Chapter Five addresses this problem in more detail. However, there's a pertinent point I need to raise now. Our economy is the cause of these problems, but more specifically our inadequate and inappropriate business measurement standard is to blame. Business has paid little attention to the environmental damage it causes in pursuit of profit because that's all it measures. A new balanced business measurement standard will hold them accountable. Until we hold them accountable at source (i.e. at the time they commit harmful practices), we are not going to address our environmental problems. We can hold global conferences on the subject and talk as much about it as we like, but until we get every business to account for their environmental impact fully, we will not solve the problem. As I mentioned earlier, CSR (Corporate Social Responsibility) reporting was supposed to address these problems, but their track record shows they have failed. They have no understanding of how our new business measurement should work (i.e. no understanding of the value creation causal model.) It's not just about environmental protection, although crucial, but about society as well. New, effective measures will go a long way in helping rectify the imbalances of the past, but there are other crucial things we need to do, which I cover in this book. Things, like stopping and redressing free market growth (Chapter Two) and developing big governments (Chapter Six), will all play an important part.

Addressing problems of post-redistribution.

Post-redistribution of wealth/value is about using taxes or other methods to redistribute wealth once it has been earned. Ideally, we should not rely on any post-redistribution methods, but have a measurement standard which encourages and supports the fair distribution of wealth/value at the time of creation. Basically, post-redistribution systems are less efficient, costly and sometimes arbitrary and therefore may have a negative impact. Here are some arguments against post-redistribution.

1. Viscount Alexis de Tocqueville (1805 - 1859) a French diplomat and political scientist wrote about American democracy noting that Americans (at the time) had a different approach to self-interest. They appreciated that to serve their own needs they had to place common good first; to ensure others needs were being served as well as their own. This is a fundamental we have all lost along the way, particularly Americans. We need to return to basic principles. A new measurement standard, based on the value creation causal model, will ensure this. It will balance the needs of all stakeholders. As a standard, it should be implemented globally, affecting everybody. Daily, people around the world will put into practice processes which consider the welfare of all, not just shareholders. Over the long-term, they will all prosper, and appreciate that putting common welfare first benefits everybody. This will change our global perspective and culture from one of greed and self-interest into one of placing common interests first. This will not make us socialists or communists, but forward-thinking Capitalists. This approach is in contrast to current methods and thinking, which serve one party's need over all others. It breeds a culture of self-interest and greed. It breaks down the most essential component which binds us as a society - trust.

Trust is a thing we have very little of today. In the past, the wealthy earned our trust and respect as they worked hard and sacrificed to achieve success. Today they earn our anger and displeasure, as most make their money through manipulative practices and deceitful propaganda, to hide the truth. They show little concern for the welfare of their fellow humans or the environment. They are society's new enemy. Their practices, systems and procedures, together with the laws and policies they helped introduced must be replaced.

2. Post redistribution of wealth/value will not restore the damage done by business processes to create wealth for shareholders in the first instance. They must be stopped at source. A new business measurement standard should achieve this. Businesses need to reconsider their options in light of common good. Environmental damage undertaken for shareholder

benefit is often irreversible. Social damage caused by business closures and wage cuts are difficult and costly to rectify.

3. Progressive tax (progressively increasing tax rates on the rich) with a high tax rate, is arbitrary and could be seen as a disincentive. If wealth/value is distributed equitably at the source, through a balanced measurement standard, this will negate the need for high tax rates. Wealth and value would be distributed more appropriately. However, in the absence of a balanced measurement standard, we are left with no other alternative than to implement a progressive tax system with a high tax rate. We would also need to tax businesses who benefit from free markets and rental incomes (among other targets highlighted in the book.)

In conclusion.

When all is said and done, it's what we do every day in business which determines what our economy is and who we are. America used to be great, when they put common good at the centre of their endeavours - then, they were true Capitalists. Now, like all other developed economies, it's all about self-interest and greed. Now we are greedy profiteers. This erodes trust and leads to inequality, which damages the economy further. This is not something we can be proud of, and neither is it efficient use of resources. Politicians wanting to "make our country great again" need to return to the basic tenets of democracy and place the interests of the majority at the centre of everything they do. Remove the laws, policies, regulations, systems and procedures which further the interests of a few over those of the majority. Getting our business measurement standard to serve the interests of all is the first step in the process.

Only when we place business on an even keel, where we consider shareholder and stakeholder needs together, can business live up to its role as an effective social tool. Only in this manner can we ensure business serves the needs of the wider community. We understand business needs to make a profit over the long-term to survive and fulfil its social duties. We also understand this will involve resolving competing demands for resources. Using a new measurement standard (like the value creation causal model) will place these competing demands in perspective, and help managers decide what's best for all, not one. Such decisions will be open to scrutiny, based on recognised procedures and best practice.

Summary.

The major contributing factor to our economic inequality is our inadequate and inappropriate business measurement standard. It focuses us on short-term profit creation for the exclusive benefit of shareholders, at the expense of other stakeholders. It's an adversarial system which unfairly favours shareholders. This makes it a profiteering system; the worst form of profiteering as it profits from its own stakeholders. It erodes trust and creates greater inequality, which damages economic growth.

It's what we do every day in business that determines what we are, not what we say we are. We are profiteers - plain and simple because that's what we do every day in business; we focus on profit exclusively. Unless we change our measurement standard to provide greater balance in serving the needs of all stakeholders, nothing changes. The alternative is for government to step in and regulate business, to ensure stakeholder interests are protected. It will also have to implement a progressive tax system with high rates to ensure a more equitable distribution of wealth. However government intervention is not the favoured route - better self-regulation is.

Chapter 2
Stop and redress free market growth.

Vested interest's first priority is to maximise profits by using an inadequate and inappropriate measurement standard, which looks after their needs, not ours. Their second priority is to extend profit opportunities within markets by removing restrictions applied by governments to protect (often vulnerable) interests. These "free markets", free from government intervention, lead to increased wealth for them.

The argument to support free markets suggests we should allow business to operate with little or no government intervention as then business functions efficiently, and can optimise profits. According to them, this benefits all as their increased wealth "trickles down" benefiting us. However, as we will learn in the next chapter, there's a fundamental flaw with this argument - it doesn't work. Little "trickles down." Therefore, providing greater, unfettered access to resources will lead to more economic enslavement and problems. So, rather than reduce government involvement, which is what "free markets" require, we need greater involvement and more (appropriate) business regulation, to protect vulnerable stakeholders from business's profiteering practices. Governments must implement laws and regulations to protect and nurture their citizens, as well as their natural resources. Vested interests want these laws and regulations discarded so they can exploit resources, to increase their wealth. What a screw-up.

In Chapter Three I explained how vested interests go about changing laws, to protect and grow their wealth. Under these circumstances, it would appear that vested interests condone, protectionism and government intervention. They would appear to be legitimate and fair practices. However, when protectionism and government intervention affects their profits, they change their tune and tell us we need "free markets" - free from government intervention and protectionism. This is a perfect example of the double standards they keep; of the hypocrisy they feed us. Expanding and protecting their wealth is their only concern. To this end they want regulations removed which hinder them from optimising profits, while installing regulations which help them optimise profits. They do all this while feeding us the lie about the virtues of free markets. By ridding themselves of government intervention and other market barriers, it ignores the good reasons they exist in the first place. They are put in place to protect citizens and national interests - the common good. Vested Interests don't concern themselves with common good, only their self-interests.

How can we allow a profiteering system to grow? If we remove protective laws and regulations, it will grow, and with it, greater economic enslavement. How can this benefit the majority? It doesn't. So, from the outset, vested interests have hidden their blatant self-interest through elaborate subterfuge, to make us believe free markets and globalisation are in our best interests when they are not.

In this chapter, we look at free markets and globalisation to uncover what a screw-up they are. We learn the frightening extent to which vested interests misinform and mislead us. How they have politicians and other influential people chanting the mantra of free markets and globalisation, oblivious to the damage they are causing their constituents.

Vested interests have done a brilliant job at hiding the cause of our most serious social, environmental, economic and business problems (namely, our inadequate and inappropriate business measurement standard.) They have done an equally good job at convincing people of the need and benefits of free markets and globalisation. This shows their power and influence, and how a change will only come about when met with mass disapproval.

Free markets - benefit or problem?
There is no such thing as a free market. Markets are influenced by politics. Regulations are set or removed according to this influence. What is of concern is whose interests are they serving. Vested interests want you to believe that markets should be free of regulations as that serves us all better. However, that just another of their lies. The wealthy rely on market regulation to protect their interests at the expense of the poor (as you will learn

in Chapter Three.) Therefore, the dilemma they face in removing unfavourable regulations, while implementing favourable ones, is how can they sell this barefaced lie to the public. They make a great fuss about removal of regulations, then by stealth and underhanded methods, they implement regulations favouring their interests.

Leaving aside their double standards and hypocrisy, let's consider the nonsense fed us to see to what extent their claims that unregulated markets are more efficient and benefit all of us. They say governments should not intervene in markets and let business get on and develop markets free from intervention as business knows best. The premise of a free market is that if left alone, markets will produce the most efficient and just outcomes. Efficient, because business knows best on how to utilise resources made available to them, and just because the competitive market process rewards individuals according to their productivity. Therefore, business should enjoy maximum freedom. If left alone, business will maximise wealth creation, thereby benefiting all society. Government intervention in the markets reduces efficiency.

Unfortunately, this premise is seriously and fundamentally flawed. The most serious flaw is to believe unregulated markets are efficient and just. If business's purpose is to maximise short-term profit, which it is, then it does not use resources efficiently but exploits resources for the benefit of its shareholders. This is neither efficient nor just use of resources. Therefore, the greater the market freedom, the greater the exploitation and unfair use of resources. Even, if your only perspective was shareholder interests, this cannot be deemed efficient use of resources. In the long-term shareholder interests are best served through adopting a balanced approach towards all stakeholders. Therefore, we can only justify free markets when business creates value for all stakeholders, including its shareholders. This means business must improve its self-regulation, through a balanced measurement standard, which ensures all business constituents (or stakeholders) are fairly and justly rewarded. Until then, we need external industry government regulations to protect the interests of all stakeholders and ensure fair distribution of wealth/value.

Theoretically, a free market should work better without intervention by external, less qualified entities. However, under the circumstances, where the stated objective of business (as dictated to by its measurement standard) is to optimise profits for the exclusive benefit of shareholders, then it will distort outcomes unfairly in their favour. Further, if there are no effect re-distribution mechanisms in place then economic inequality will skyrocket. Therefore, we need somebody, or something, to intervene to ensure fairness and balance. We do not make available national or global resources exclusively to benefit a few. How can the worst form of profiteering (profiteering from one's own stakeholders) be fair, just, or reasonable? It's the complete opposite. That's why it's the root cause of our most serious social, environmental, economic and business problems. Why allow this dreadful system to exploit resources in an unrestrained fashion?

Free market repeal.
Therefore, the biggest argument against free markets is that business does not have any effective self-regulatory measures (i.e. we have no balanced measurement standard, which looks after the well being of all stakeholders.) We allow shareholders to exploit local, national and even global resources for their exclusive benefit. We have no effective, inbuilt means of redistributing this wealth/value. Further, there are no mechanisms in place to stop or limit harmful practices from happening; practices employed for the myopic purpose of creating wealth for shareholders. Practices harmful to both society and the environment.

So, without effective, self-regulated business, we need much greater government intervention to ensure we utilise resources for the benefit of all. We clearly cannot leave this to our profit-obsessed business leaders, who through the process do not care about the harm and difficulty they cause, all in the name of self-interest, and greed.

So, under these circumstances, we cannot limit government intervention to wealth redistribution through higher corporate and income tax on the wealthy. Neither can we limit it to protecting the long-term interests of society, by protecting workers, the environment, suppliers, and wider community (thereby ensuring business lives up to its social responsibilities.) Governments must become more involved in economic activity, providing support to business (a subject discussed in greater detail in subsequent chapters.) So, rather than having free markets free from government intervention, there needs to be far greater government involvement, for the benefit of everybody, including business. Regulations must serve the common good, or be removed.

Without effective business self-regulation, government must not only halt the advance of free markets but start repealing laws and regulations protecting only shareholder needs. They must start introducing new laws and regulations which protect workers, environment, community and other stakeholders.

They tell us that this will drive business away, but this is untrue. By rewarding all fairly and justly, through a balanced approach, builds a strong, active economy from which all benefit. On the other hand, progressively weakening the economy through unfair, imbalanced practices, results in poorer returns and higher risk for business. Fairness and balance, are the two key elements for long-term success, not unfair, unjust and imbalanced practices.

Vested interests often threaten us, if we increase taxes or if we "interfere", making trading more difficult (in their opinion,) they will relocate or reduce their investment. Free markets make this a reality where they can hold us to ransom to their profiteering demands. They can easily relocate somewhere else in the world but still sell to us under the same terms and conditions. In this way, they get their way at the expense of all others. The purpose of greater government intervention is not to "hurt business" - the complete opposite. All we want to see is the fair distribution of wealth/value, for the long-term benefit of all. Vested interests only concern is short-term profit for shareholders. Increasing government regulations should make relocation of businesses difficult as they are unlikely to gain access to the market they vacate on the same terms and conditions. They will have to think long and hard about their decisions. By having strong government involvement, we can grow strong national economies over the long-term, which will be highly attractive to business. We have to get rid of this fixation on short-term profits in favour of a balanced long-term view of all stakeholder needs.

Free market - the future.

As already explained, government needs to become bigger and more active in business. Despite certain limitations (such as, the "heavy hand" of government, which I will explain shortly) democratic governments are best at reconciling conflicting demands within society and, more importantly, for improving our collective well-being (or quality-of-life.) They have to become fully involved and take the broader decisions affecting economic life. Governments should provide the operational frameworks for every economic activity, for without this, business is free to exploit markets, with disastrous consequences for others. Every single chapter in this book is about greater government involvement; calling for and expecting government to support and/or institute much of the change. After all, they are the lawmakers and have the well-being of society at heart. The changes proposed in this book are essentially about improving living standards and quality-of-life for all, while also protecting the environment. To do that, governments must become bigger and more active in business. Shrinking government involvement leads precisely to the problems we now face. Left unaddressed, reduced government "intervention" could lead to anarchy.

The reality is, less government intervention can only become a possibility when we have effective self-regulated businesses, achieved through introducing a balanced measurement standard. However, self-regulation will only go some way, not all the way in meeting societies needs. For example, governments need to provide a supportive environment within which business can work successfully. So, we require greater government involvement in business, not less.

So, "free markets" are nonsense, but under vastly improved, and effective self-regulation, there may be a case for slightly less government intervention. When business follows the dictates of a new, balanced measurement standard, it would be in a good position to judge society's needs. Under such circumstances, the free market argument may be valid, but until then it's not. A government is more likely to apply a "heavy hand," i.e. apply a general approached best suited for "normal circumstances." Not all situations are "normal", so business is best suited to decide, but only when business operates as an effective social tool, looking after the interests of all, not just shareholders. It's ridiculous to give business a free hand when they operate in their own self-interest, not those of society. Until then, the concept of "free markets" is nothing more than a cheap ruse, for vested interests to remove obstacles in their path of greater wealth creation - What A Screw-Up!

The dangers of free markets.

Commonsense should warn us that when markets are free from regulations, unscrupulous behaviour will occur, particularly in an economy which encourages and rewards selfish behaviour. We are profiteers, so when we remove regulations and make it a free-for-all, expect the worst. What would our society become if we abolished all laws - lawless. Who would suffer - the innocent, law-abiding majority. The same applies to our economy. Remove the laws and regulations and you are left to the mercy of unscrupulous individuals. Don't expect any mercy. The 2008 financial crisis is proof of this. Financial markets were deregulated, and this deregulation led directly to this crisis. It led to governments bailing out their banks who adopted risky and predatory tactics which ultimately saw their demise. The cost was borne by taxpayers, not Bankers who walked away almost unscathed. Free markets allowed a previously conservative, stalwart of the economy to become a predatory, self-serving entity which justifiably earned the ire and distrust of the populace. Who is to blame? Government and regulatory bodies. They hold the reins, and they let them go. This is evidence of the degree to which governments and regulatory bodies are manipulated by vested interests - the wealthy one per cent.

Despite billions being pumped into banks and serious malpractices noted, nobody was held accountable. To the person-in-the-street, governments failed them by allowing banks to behave as they did, and not to hold anybody accountable. This feeling of unfairness, of one set of rules for Bankers and another for us, leads to a feeling of betrayal. This feeling is justifiable, because, we have been betrayed. The political system failed to serve the majority, who appointed them on the proviso they serve our needs.

Politics is the battleground where decisions on how to divide the economic pie are lost or won. The war is being won by the wealthy one per cent. This represents a betrayal of the trust we place in our politicians to serve our needs. There is an enormous role for government to play in correcting (regulating) markets, by ensuring they work for the benefit of the majority. Deregulated markets are inefficient as they tend to work for those pulling the strings of the economy - the one per cent. We depend on politicians not to betray the trust we place in them. For this, they must be held accountable. You must hold your MP accountable.

Another unpleasant aspect related to the deregulation of the financial sector is it creates greater risk. The wealthy are able to handle risk better than the poor. This enables them to capitalise on the poor's weakness. The poor lose their assets, which are acquired by the rich at below market value. We need regulations to stop this type of practice, not deregulation which encourages it.

Free markets and globalisation - public enemy number one.

The practice of globalisation before the introduction of the World Trade Organisation (WTO) in 1995 was benign. It involved the trade between nations of the world. Trade agreements were negotiated on an individual, quid pro quo basis. Since the establishment of the WTO its taken on a malignant meaning and approach. Globalisation now is about the development of an unregulated global economy. Globalisation scales up the problems of free markets, applying them to global markets. It takes a bad idea and scales it up, making it even worse. To be part of this globalised market, you must adopt their free-market principles and rules. This weakens nation-states as they must forgo the regulations which protect their economy, citizens and resources.

There is no question about it, the removal of regulations facilitates easy trading, and this benefits those businesses involved. However, it ignores the good reason nation states had regulations in place in the first instant and denies them the right to impose regulations in the future. They have no mechanism to protect their own interests and are left naked to the unscrupulous and self-serving interests of the wealthy one per cent. The people who are behind this new deregulated globalisation.

If markets become "globalised," free and unregulated, then business can make products anywhere (as cheaply as possible) and sell them everywhere because all markets are free and open. This is good news for those business involved - huge international markets and low production costs mean far better profits. It also means increased negotiation power over national states, which lead to lower taxes. There is no question - globalisation is good for businesses involved, but right now what's good for business is not good for national economies and their citizens. In fact, it's darn right harmful. The only people who benefit are the wealthy one per cent. Everybody else pays the price.

Unfortunately, politicians, among others, are influenced by the nonsense fed them about the virtues of free markets and globalisation. They get behind the concept and beat the drum for vested interests. I can only assume they do so in ignorance or, perhaps they have a vested interest themselves. Business in its current form is about self-interest (shareholder interests) nothing else. Government's interests are about the well-being of all citizens (common good.) How can globalisation and free markets (or self-interest) align with government objectives (or common good)? They don't. They represent the antithesis of government objectives. As a consequence, government regulations to protect citizens interests are taken away so national resources may benefit the self-interest of a small minority.

Globalisation has weakened developed economies through the loss of manufacturing (too low labour cost countries), and poor protection of local workers, loss of common assets, erosion of national interests, among other problems. This is the objective of globalisation - the breaking down of national states, replacing them with an economic order run by huge transnationals. Economics is supposed to shape our future through global markets, free from narrow national interests and inhibiting regulations.

Really, how did they manage to sell such drivel in the first place? On the one hand, vested interests tell us governments must not interfere with business (as business knows best on running business), but it's quite all right for business to shape our future. Surely, following their logic and reasoning, governments know best on running government. Businesses know little about government, so business should not interfere in running governments? Imagine a society run by huge transnationals, who operate on the principle of the survival of the fittest. A government has to look after all its citizens. The care and support provided to its weakest and most vulnerable reflects good governance. The effective functioning of government does not suit economic systems and never will. We need greater government involvement to protect national interests and provide a supportive infrastructure so that national economies can grow and prosper and provide a good quality-of-life for all. We don't grow and prosper through dismantling national economies. Free markets and globalisation are a nation state's worst enemy. They want government power reduced.

The price of globalisation.

Below is a partial list of the cost of globalisation. It's neither comprehensive or detailed, but sufficient to show it's undesirable and does not serve the citizens of nation states. The pros of globalisation are that it serves the wealthy very well. Increased economic inequality is proof of this. Unfortunately, what's good for the wealthy is not good for society as they have corrupted and manipulated the system to work for them.

1. Governments lose their negotiating power.

When businesses can relocate anywhere in the world to produce, yet still sell their products under the same terms and conditions as if they were manufactured locally, they have the upper hand in negotiating with national governments. This leads to lower taxes and increased corporate welfare in the form of concessions.

2. Government loses taxes.

Transnationals manage to manipulate tax regulations to escape paying taxes on income earned in a particular country. Proxy amounts are declared locally, with the bulk of earnings ending up in tax havens, where little or no tax is paid.

3. Governments go into decline.

The object of free markets is to see the size of government reduced. The assault on government occurs at both a national and global level. This does not serve citizens needs. It leads to the lowering of their quality-of-life.

4. Democracy is threatened.

Globalisation adds to economic inequality. Inequality cannot be allowed to grow any larger and neither can it persist for much longer. Inequality is injustice and injustice has a short fuse. People who know, or believe the system does not serve their needs, may take radical steps to address the problem.

5. People lose their jobs.

Manufacturing moves to low labour cost countries. Developed economies lose jobs.

6. Job losses lower wages across the board.

As more people are chasing fewer jobs, this puts downward pressure on wages across the board.

7. Weakens the effectiveness of labour unions.

Job losses mean fewer union members, and with increasing demand on the remaining jobs, employers often insist on employing non-unionised employees.

8. A weak labour market encourages a flexible labour market.

A flexible labour market is one in which employees are required to work flexible hours, retrain for new skills, relocate geographically to retain their job and to accept performance related pay. It's a concept promoted by vested interests and claimed to contribute to a stronger economy. This claim depends on what you mean by a "stronger economy". If you mean an economy which serves the rich, then the statement is true, but if you mean an economy which serves workers, then it's definitely incorrect. Not all aspects of a flexible labour market are bad, but when you consider the rationale behind it, it's bad. It's about shifting cost and risk onto employees. Employees are, in most cases, ill-equipped to bear the cost and risks of business. It's unfair and unreasonable to burden them, with no additional reward, apart from retaining their jobs. It is a form of labour abuse, couched in a language meant to mislead us. Labour should be protected and nurtured. This leads to a highly motivated and engaged labour force; one more committed and loyal to their employer. A labour force willing to invest in themselves and their job.

9. Natural and strategic resources are unprotected.

Transnationals have access to natural resources and strategic industries, from which they profit. This is a serious threat to national states long-term prosperity and security. They must protect resources and control/provide strategically important industries and infrastructure. The very fabric of nation states is being eroded for profit, by a few.

10. Forces financial market liberalisation.

The Financial Services Agreement of the World Trade Organisation (WTO) forces financial market liberalisation (another name for free markets) onto countries. This restrains them from imposing regulations which would ensure their financial systems are stable and serve their economy and society the way it should.

Globalisation is about a system working for the benefit of a few, not about the welfare of the majority.

What's wrong with Trump's call to "Make America Great"? What's wrong with him calling for the return of jobs to America lost through declining American manufacture (or globalisation?) All he is trying to do is protect the American economy and reverse the damaging effects of free markets and globalisation. Only those who benefit from free markets and globalisation are complaining. When you have read Chapters Six and Nine, you will appreciate more fully the damaging affects free markets and globalisation are having. It will make you realise popularism is simply the populace rising against economic inequality, the cause of their rapidly falling quality-of-life. Unfair practices lead to the growth of popularism.

Summary.

Markets need regulation to protect stakeholders from poor business self-regulation, which only looks after the needs of shareholder interests. This means resources are not efficiently or justly used, but rather inappropriately, to enrich a few. Therefore, to remove regulations will spread the problem further, hurting society and environment. Of course, we want business to succeed, but not under the current regime. They must get their house in order and start using resources, which we make available to them, in a fair and just way.

Until business drastically improves its self-regulation, thereby ensuring it serves the needs of all stakeholders, we must stop free market development (i.e. markets with fewer regulations.) We should, in fact, start reversing the process by revisiting markets where they removed restrictions/limitations to see if they adversely affected workers, communities and the environment, or any other stakeholder. Where appropriate, reintroduce them.

The best solution is better self-regulation, but if this is not to be, then governments must step in and actively reintroduce laws and regulations to protect national interests. Over the long-term, this will grow the economy, contrary to what vested interests tell us.

Whether business self-regulates better or governments step in and regulate the markets more effectively, government's role in business must increase beyond this regulatory role. Government must provide the vision and support to strengthen the economy. By reducing this critical government role will see the economy of the future shrink, to the detriment of all. Government may not know how to run individual businesses well - that's not their purpose, but they have an essential role to play in shaping and supporting economic development. They also have an important role in protecting the interests of the majority from unscrupulous practices. Governments know what's best for national interests, not global markets, overseen by transnationals.

Free markets and globalisation want to see government's role reduced, but thankfully there's time to reverse this ill-conceived ideology.

Chapter 3
Stop and redress rentier economy growth.

What's driving economic inequality should now be evident. We manage business using financial measures which optimise shareholder wealth, at the expense of all others. We then strip away protective laws and regulations so vested interests can generate even more profit from "free markets." Again, this is done at the expense of all others. This wealth does not "trickle down" to benefit all as claimed. Wealth, taken from others, through poor economic systems, accumulates at the top. As a consequence, economic inequality increases. Because of these, and other entrenched systems, it is likely that inequality will continue to increase in the future.

The two factors mentioned earlier are by no means the only contributors to inequality, but they are significant. Most of the increased wealth they generate is not reinvested in our "active" economy but redirected out into the "rentier" economy, to the detriment of our "active" economy and most of us. Investing in the "rentier" economy benefits them, and harms us. So, making the wealthy richer hurts the average citizen - it does not help them. In fact, they use increasing inequality to benefit themselves. "Trickle down" is a hoax to make us believe wealth will be spread equitably. It was supposed to "even things out" so we all benefited. In reality, they knew it would never work, that it would have the opposite effect. They knew by increasing inequality they would increase middle/low income financial vulnerabilities, which they could then capitalise on - the "Vacuum Up" effect. What makes this hoax so egregious, is its deviousness. They create vulnerabilities, under the pretence of this lie, which they then profit from.

In this chapter, I will elaborate on the economic and social problems caused by inequality and the problems the rentier economy creates. I will also elaborate on the "trickle down" hoax and the "Vacuum Up" effect, which lies behind the hoax.

Economic inequality not the problem - the scale is.
Individuals are becoming super rich against a backdrop of increasing government debt. This screams at us - something is chronically wrong with how we distribute wealth. Bear in mind; these individuals make their money by trading in the countries whose governments have high debt. These countries and their citizens should be the major beneficiaries of this trading, not the individual. Unfortunately, this is not the case. Our systems favour the rich. They grow richer while governments grow poorer, as do their citizens. So the greater the divide - the greater the hardship felt by the majority. This leads to serious social problems: that's bad enough, but the problems don't end there. The wealthier an individual, the more money they direct out of our "active" economy into the "rentier" economy, weakening our active economy. That's bad news for the average person, whose well-being relies on a strong, active economy.

In an attempt to mislead us, and cover up the harm caused by unfair wealth distribution, vested interests tell us not to worry. They claim the accumulated wealth held in the hands of a few benefits us as it eventually "trickles down" to benefit all. Another useless phrase they use to explain the benefits of the rich getting richer, is, "a rising tide lifts all boats in the harbour." I'm not sure how this works in economic terms, but then little they say makes much sense. We are also told to be careful not to upset this balance. We must allow the rich to get richer, or we will remove the incentive for them to invest, and as a result, we will all suffer.

As we learnt in Chapter Two, they tell us that government should not interfere with business. Let it get on and make profits with little or no interference from government. This "free market" approach serves us all by letting business do what it's supposed to, and that's make profits because that's what eventually benefits all. Let the rich get richer. Remember the rising tide analogy?

Sound reasonable to you? Quick question - if trickle down is working, why is there such a chasm between rich and poor and why is it widening? Why is wealth shifting from the hands of the government into the hands of wealthy individuals? One reason is our tax systems are now regressive where (effectively) the rich pay less pro rata than the poor. We should have a progressive tax where the rich pay a higher pro rata rate, and that rate should be set high at over seventy per cent. This issue is dealt with later in the book. As the tax system favours the rich, the only thing we can rely on to redistribute wealth is trickle down. This must rank as the dumbest thing on earth - a major screw-up. Not only does it not work, but it also works in reverse, vacuuming up what little wealth the poor have, into the hands of ridiculously rich people.

By allowing a disproportionate concentration of wealth to accumulate in the hands of the rich, causes severe harm to our economy and society, not good. This is what we will look at in this chapter - the damage done by allowing a few to hold too much wealth. There will always be a rich/poor divide. This isn't bad, in fact, it shows things are working correctly in our economy. It shows there are successful businesses and their shareholders are reaping the benefits. However, a chasm represents a problem. It shows things are not working correctly.

We need successful businesses. They need to generate long-term profits to succeed. As they succeed, so, a rich class emerges. However, they must share their success with other stakeholders. Unfortunately, this is not the case. Therefore, we must not give businesses access to resources for the exclusive benefit of shareholders, but for all. If business does not improve its self-regulation, ensuring it works for all stakeholders not just shareholders, then governments have to become more vigorously involved. They will have to legislate to protect other stakeholders interests and increase corporate taxes and tax on the wealthy, to ensure fair wealth distribution. We cannot rely on stupid fallacies like trickle down - very little trickles down. The percentage of wealth/value which trickles down as a per cent of what's created renders the concept useless. It's a lie and a horrible hoax. The prospect of post-event government involvement is also not ideal, as the damage caused by business's myopic profit focus has already been done. Other opportunities are lost as explained in Chapter One. We need proactive business self-regulation to prevent damage in the first place. We need a new business measurement standard to stop the problems of poor wealth/value distribution and harmful processes at the source. We must also stop free market growth as it only benefits the rich.

The negative social consequences of the rich/poor divide.

It is highly likely that because of entrenched systems, practices and procedures now in place, we are in the invidious position where we face the prospect of ever-increasing economic inequality. This will take us back in time, away from hard-earned equality, to an era of "lord and master." However, in today's society, it will be increasingly difficult to hide such gross inequality. It's a potential social time-bomb. These social problems are potentially more harmful than the economic effects, which are bad enough. Economic inequality continues to grow to nobody's advantage. The rich are blinkered by their success, but things could turn nasty for them quickly. You can only abuse a system for so long before the final straw. I don't condone violence in any shape or form in addressing the problem, but rather the establishment of a fairer economic system which serves all. Inequality has a short fuse.

We know the wealthy one per cent are getting richer by using our inadequate and inappropriate measurement standard and free markets. They are also getting richer because we do not tax them appropriately, indicated through the increasing wealth of individuals and rising government debt. Wealth is shifting from the hands of the government into the hands of individuals. There are two reasons for this.

First, the richer people become, the more powerful they become. The more powerful they are, the more pressure they apply on governments, regulatory bodies and every entity which can help or harm their cause. They threaten us saying that if we tax them too heavily we remove the incentive to invest and we will all suffer as a consequence. Politicians believe this nonsense and crumble under pressure. We know these claims to be baseless and untrue. The result is we shift the tax burden elsewhere, to those who can ill afford it. Even if the tax burden is not shifted, government revenues will decline. Whatever the outcome, the consequence is a lowering of the quality-of-life for most. The rich/poor divide widens.

Second, the rich are good at tax avoidance. They can afford to employ expensive lawyers and accountants to exploit every possible loophole to avoid paying tax. Tax avoidance is legal (evasion is not.) However, the greater the rich/poor divide, the greater the portion of revenue which escapes taxation. This results in governments shifting the tax burden down the line to the less well-off and those who can ill afford further financial burden. So while tax avoidance is legal, it's hardly moral, as it's only available to a few who can afford it. It's a widespread practice which includes certain members of the Royal Family. Some have no shame in admitting it – they even boast about it. We will always have a rich/poor divide, but the bigger it is, the more money escapes the tax net as these mechanisms are not available to the average person. Either we stop the generation of excessive profit at its source (through a new measurement standard), or we tax the rich more progressively.

Another problem caused by the one per cent's insatiable drive for wealth, (which leads to this widening gap,) is the rising mountain of consumer debt. Vested interest "engineer" this debt as they have no qualms in keeping wage/salary increases below that of inflation and dismantle the power of trade unions, to curb the costs of labour. As a result, real incomes have been in steady decline for decades, with a resultant drop in quality-of-life. However, this drop in disposable income presents vested interests with a problem – consumers have less money to spend. This means lower sales and lower profits. To counter this, they provide easy credit and allow the average citizen to rack up massive debt. For this, they charge exorbitant rates. This adds to the average person's costs, lowering their quality-of-life even further. This is a hugely lucrative market for the financial sector. It's a win-win for vested interests and a double whammy for the average worker, making life much harder for them. Debt problems are a significant social problem. This is part of the vacuum-up effect, explained later.

The decline in real incomes over the decades has led to a further problem. Research has proved that we can link social mobility directly to that of one's parents wealth. As real incomes have been in steady decline, so too has this adversely affected the social mobility of their offspring. This is highly unjust and damaging to the economy, for which we all suffer.

Another fundamental reason the rich are getting richer quicker is that money makes money. Capital returns outstrip economic growth, so those who are already rich get richer quicker. On the other hand, the average person depends on economic growth to dictate their incomes. A further reason to ensure we distribute wealth/value more fairly at the source, to help lift all.

Research has found that if we do not share economic gains, worker productivity declines. This is not surprising. If you do not reward somebody fairly, they will reluctantly support you in the future, if at all. The greater the inequality, the greater the resentment and productivity loss. A drop in worker productivity equates to a drop in quality-of-life, as workers don't feel they are appreciated any more and no longer enjoy their jobs. What's more, rising inequality erodes the trust workers have towards employers and their willingness to cooperate. This leads to wider distrust and dismay with the system, not just with their employer.

The wider the divide between rich and poor, the higher the social discord. People who are battling to meet their everyday needs, facing a steady fall in quality-of-life, start questioning the opulence of a few. How can an economic system serve these few so well, yet leave many hard-working people worse off, year on year? This ultimately leads to social unrest and upheaval, which probably won't serve the rich well. We have already witnessed the start of unrest in the form of the "Occupy Movement" and more recently, the "Yellow Jacket Movement" in France. The more government austerity affects the middle-class, the more vociferous public discord becomes. This discord is the foundation of "popularism". Trust is the glue which holds society together. It's fading fast and for good reason.

The problems of an expanding rentier economy.
A strong middle class is a good indication of a healthy economy as their income is recirculated quickly and almost in its entirety within what I call our "active economy." In other words, their disposable income is negligible; it's all consumed by living costs. Adam Smith (the "father" of modern economics) identified three forms of income - profit, wages and rent. Profit and wages are earned in our "active economy." The owners of capital and labour have to do something to earn a profit and wage respectively (i.e. they are active participants in the economy making and selling things.) However, rental income does not involve active participation; it involves the transfer of money from one party to another based on one party's ownership of a scarce resource. For example, the owners of property undertake no active role in the economy. They receive an income from their scarce resource. Therefore, it would be inaccurate to include their income with that of the active economy as it involves no productive output. Thus, we allocate it to what we refer to as the "rentier economy."

As the rich only consume a small portion of their income (i.e. their disposable income is high,) they generally invest their disposable income in the rentier economy. This is because the risk is (often) lower and returns higher than the active economy. Money earned in the active economy but withdrawn from it weakens it. This is not good for most of us as a shrinking active economy ultimately affects all society. We depend on the active economy for our incomes.

When we weaken our active economy (through fund withdrawal), investment returns decline, with a proportionate increase in risk. This, in turn, results in even more funds leaving the active economy and ending up in the rentier economy, thereby accelerating the downward cycle.

For the above reasons the claim made by the rich that if we tax them more, or introduce further regulations, they won't invest in the "active" economy, is complete nonsense. Politicians appear to believe the disinformation fed to them by the wealthy, and are influenced by them, reducing taxes, and removing regulations. This increases their wealth which they then invest in the rentier economy - to our disadvantage. If taxed harder, and regulated more, more money would remain in the active economy, thus making it a more attractive investment (through growth.) As a result of which, the active, rather than the rentier economy, would attract vested interest's investment.

Once funds enter the rentier economy, they often become "dead funds" unlikely to return to the active (or productive) economy, for the following reasons. The rentier economy is innovation and risk-averse, so once funds end up in this economy, they are unlikely to return to the active economy, which is dependant on innovation for returns. While innovation holds the potential for high rewards, it is equally risky. So once funds enter the rentier economy, they stay there because of the adverse risk/return factor. Many investors are risk averse. This inhibits the active economy and its ability to grow and attract funds back.

It's not just about property.

When I refer to the rentier economy, you must realise this does not only include income generated from property but from a vast, and ever-expanding source of "scarce" resources. This includes control of natural resources and intellectual property, which incorporates copyright, trademarks, trade secrets and patents. While there are many benefits to be had in developing intellectual property for the active economy, problems arise in their excessive protection. These often well exceed the investment and risk undertaken in the first instance and become a massive profit generator for vested interests and the rentier economy. The irony of this is that the wealthy one per cent calls for free markets as they claim they don't want government involvement, yet they push for greater legislation to protect their intellectual property. What hypocrites! Excessive protection limits the spread of knowledge, an essential element for expanding our active economy, for the benefits of all. Patents are not designed to improve innovation, but to increase rents. Patents are a monopoly. Monopolies represent rent generating activities.

Consider this, in 2012 over 2.3 million patents were registered - more than double that of 1995. That was the year they introduced the World Trade Organisation's Agreement on Trade-

Related aspects on International Property Rights (TRIPS). Before that, many countries had no patent laws or only gave patent holders a few years of protection. Now countries have excessive patent laws, protecting patent holders for 20 years or more. Patent laws and other laws protecting IC (Intellectual Capital) are necessary. They only become problematic when extended for unfavourably long periods, merely to enrich their owners, at the expense of benefiting the broader community.

Extending copyright laws is another area of concern. In the past, creators did not push copyright, but with publisher involvement, copyright protection has increased substantially. It went from fourteen up to fifty years for literary works and is rising in many countries to over 70 years after the death of the author.

Royalties have also increased massively for music, film, video, and computer games, plus other similar products. In the European Union sound recording protection has risen to 70 years and 95 years in the USA. The World Intellectual Property Organisation (WIPO) claims that in some countries copyright-intensive industries are more profitable than construction, transport and mining and that their incomes are rising rapidly. It's all about business greed. The wealthy one per cent push for excessive protection while telling us we need free markets while relying on government intervention (in the form of excessive protectionist laws) to optimise their profits.

The darker side of the rentier economy.
Rental activities don't stop there. Money lending is another form of rental activity. While it is a necessary mechanism for our economy, it's often abused when businesses charge exorbitant interest rates for payday loans and other forms of similar credit, targeting and exploiting the most vulnerable. These businesses are harmful to society. This requires stringent usury regulation and review of long-term consumer debts. People are falling into the debt trap because wages have stagnated in the face of rising costs and cuts in government support, because of our dysfunctional economic systems.

While payday loans are an obvious credit abuser, needing tight regulation and strict usury laws, credit card lending is hardly much better. I think the following aptly describes the actions of the rich. "With one hand they taketh away, and with the other, they taketh away." They take away with one hand by limiting wage/salary increases. They then provide easy credit, to ensure their sales and profits don't suffer. In providing this credit they knowingly "taketh away" through unreasonably high interests rates, far higher than other businesses earn. This adds to people's cost and increases inequality. However, this is something we have come to expect from the financial sector - untrustworthy, unscrupulous, profiteers. A far cry from their old image of conservative, trustworthy, businesses with scruples. Consider this, for a minimal amount of work and investment credit card companies make more profits from their fees than supermarket retailers make from the complex job of running an extensive distribution and selling network, making a wide variety of essential products available to the public at the lowest prices. As a consequence, personal debt in developed economies is increasing. Credit is an important tool, but it can, and is, abused. The government can stop this through tighter regulations.

On-line gambling is another insidious form of rental activity, causing social hardship, but allowed to grow because a few can enrich themselves at the expense of others, often vulnerable people. Our first priority should be to protect the vulnerable and weak, otherwise what society are we? Gambling activities increase when people see little or no opportunity to improve their lives. Gambling, in their view, provides a possible "way out" of hardship. Worsening inequality drives greater gambling. It's precisely these people who should not be gambling. The wealthy one per cent create the conditions which drive them to gamble, and then they capitalise on these poor peoples worsening plight. They make huge fortunes from these naive people - vacuuming up every morsel from the poor man's table. Look at the obscene earnings taken by Denise Coates, CEO of Bet 365, who earned an income of £265million in 2018. That's equivalent to £726,000 per day. To make matters even worse, a large part of gambling is funded via credit cards. This practice has to be stopped. Only the gaming and credit card companies win, while society has to pick up the tab.

The many ugly facets of rent.

Apart from the exploitative, dark side, there are many unpleasant guises taken on by rent-seeking activities. One form of rent-seeking is for a person to take a higher portion of wealth (or profit) than would otherwise have been produced without their effort. So CEOs (Chief Executive Officers) who take huge bonuses, engage in rent-seeking practices. This form of rent-seeking and profiteering are similar. Profiteering occurs when an unfair advantage is used to achieve a higher profit than would otherwise be expected. That's the same in this case. The person uses some leverage (an unfair advantage) to take a greater share of the profit than they created. They are profiteers. Both profiteering and this form of rent-seeking are about the unfair transfer of funds. It's one of the worst forms of rent-seeking as it's unjustified and therefore unfair. Chapter Four explains, in more detail why executive pay in large corporations is entirely unjustified and harmful and how it can be stopped.

Factors which bolster the rentier economy.

There are certain actions taken by governments which inadvertently fuel the growth of the rentier economy. We need to be aware of these so we can make informed decisions, which will benefit the majority, not the rich. Two examples are estate tax and capital gain tax. The rich have influenced government to lower tax rates on these, to protect their wealth. We now need to reverse this for the following reasons.

By lowering estate taxes (which should only apply to the wealthy), families are encouraged to retain and grow their wealth. This perpetuates economic inequality and all the disadvantages associated with it. This denies governments the opportunity to redistribute wealth more equitably and halt the inequality cycle. It also reduces philanthropic activities as there's less incentive for them to give their money away. They want to retain as much of their wealth as possible to pass on. If they can't pass it on (because of taxes), they give it away to "good causes," rather than the government, who in their opinion, squander money on looking after the common good. Really - what next? By lowering estate taxes, the wealthy retain a considerable portion of their wealth in the rentier economy, as its secure and returns are high. Higher estate taxes would return money to the active economy where it benefits all, including the wealthy. The same logic applies to capital gain taxes. Lower taxes reduces government revenues which would have been spent in the active economy, for the benefit of all. Instead, retained wealth is redirected out of the active economy into the rentier economy.

Outdated institutions form part of the rentier economy.

By ignoring calls to modernise and simplify certain institutions, they contribute to the rentier economy. Our judicial system is a case in point. Our judicial system needs to be simplified, and the legal process sped up. Unless we do that, it remains too costly for the majority to access. It's no longer "justice for all" but "justice for the wealthy." By limiting the majority's access to the legal system leaves them disadvantaged and vulnerable to abuse. That's like the apartheid era in South Africa, where Black South Africans had limited access to the courts compared to their White counterparts.

Our judicial institution is maintained by design. It benefits the wealthy one per cent. They use the cost of legal processes as a form of protection/intimidation. Calls to modernise and simplify, fall on deaf ears. Having a compromised legal system hinders economic growth, an issue addressed in Chapter Seven. The point I wanted to make here is that when you have a system which is designed to be cumbersome, slow-moving and overly complicated, it operates as a monopoly. Monopolies represent rent-seeking activities as they take unearned profits. It involves the transfer of wealth from one to another without productive outlay. Any system designed to be deliberately slow-moving and unnecessarily complicated creates rent, because of the complexities. The complexity and inefficiencies represent rent. This applies to all cumbersome, slow moving institutions, not just our judicial institution.

"Technology disrupters" contribute to the rentier economy.

Many of the so-called "technology disrupters" such as Just Eat, Deliveroo, Airbnb and Uber don't actually provide the services they sell, they are merely a platform for ordering them. Consequently, they don't incur the costs or risk associated with providing such services, but charge high commission rates for providing a relatively inexpensive service. That means they are taking an unearned slice of the pie - the unearned portion represents rent. It explains why these businesses are valued so highly. Their high returns of a low cost/risk base have enabled them to monopolise markets. This trend will continue, and thus their rent-seeking practices will grow, to the majority's disadvantage.

The problems these "disrupters" introduce are not just to be found in their rent-seeking activities, but in the way they attempt to skirt regulations. Their approach appears to be to ignore regulations and wait until they are caught. They then plead ignorance, or that it's not their responsibility, they are "only a technology platform, nothing else." Of course, that's entirely incorrect, they are more than a technology platform and need to accept responsibility for the consequences of their actions. This all goes to reinforce the need for more regulation and bigger government to hold these "play it lose and fast entrepreneurs." We will consider some of these regulatory breaches later on in the relevant chapters, together with the problems they cause.

Middle-class rental "empires."

The rich are not alone in exploiting the rentier economy. The affluent middle-class use it as well. Most people understand that property capital growth is good and that property is a safe investment. As a result, there has been a growth in so-called "wealth coaches" who for a tidy fee "coach" affluent middle-class people on how to capitalise on the "Buy-To-Rent" property market. They explain how they can use their property to get a mortgage on a second property with good rental potential. After a few years, they acquire a third property using their two properties as security. And so they keep repeating this process, adding to their property portfolio, until they own many properties.

Socially and financially this is a bad practice for governments, and therefore, for you and I. Again, like all rentier investments, they are taking money away from the active economy. However, this introduces its own set of problems. It helps inflate property prices and makes it difficult for first-time buyers to enter the market. This, often, condemns them to renters-for-life. In turn, this creates problems for governments when these people come to retire. The government will have to provide pensions/support which will cover inflated rents to house them during their retirement. Everybody should have a right to own their property. This provides security in later life and minimises the financial burden placed on the government. Governments could spend the cost of housing "renters-for-life" in retirement, more wisely, elsewhere. The wealthy put governments under pressure to allow multiple property ownership, as it's an easy and secure source of income for them. However, in the long-term the government and the poor "foot the bill". It's an incredibly short-sighted practice, which is very easy to stop. Progressively tax multiple properties, making the ownership of three or more properties uneconomical.

There's another side to this property market. As incomes have stagnated over the years and because easy credit has enabled families to "balance" their budgets, families financial position is much worse off. Simultaneously, the previously mentioned "Buy-To-Rent" practice drives house prices up. As a consequence, house affordability is progressively slipping further out of reach for the average family.

The Vacuum Up effect.
As you have gathered throughout this chapter, "trickle down" is a concept which does not work. Take Denise Coates (CEO of Bet 365) as an example, she's worth almost three billion pounds, accumulated in under eighteen years. Not much of her wealth has trickled down, yet her business alone vacuums up over £2.5 billion a year from ordinary people, the ninety-nine per cent. Her clients are encouraged to gamble because our economic systems no longer serve their needs. What about credit card companies

who also capitalise on the ninety-nine per cent's worsening financial position. They do particularly well out of them. Very little of their owner's wealth trickles down either. What of pay-day loan providers? Let's also not forget about landlords, who capitalise on people who cannot afford their own homes because the economic system no longer serves them. You get the picture - our economic systems do not serve the majority, this places them in a financial predicament they should not be in. They have to borrow money and gamble as "a way out." People prey on these difficulties, "vacuuming up" every penny they have, and even pennies they don't, by pushing them further into debt.

Before reading this book, you've probably heard about "trickle down", as it's a process proclaimed from the hilltops as an effective redistribution mechanism. It goes hand-in-hand with the reason we are told we should allow the rich to get richer. Once they've made their fortunes, it trickles down, and we are all substantially better off. Really! Whoever promotes this idea is at best delusional. Delusion is something we could live with, but this is not about delusion, but devious and manipulative design.

From the outset, vested interests appreciated little (as a percentage of wealth created) would trickle down; it would accumulate at the top. This would create economic scarcity in the middle/low-income groups. This weakens them and makes them vulnerable to abuse. They knew they could then create systems, practices and methods to prey on these people's vulnerabilities. The principle behind "vacuum up" is to create scarcity and with it, weakness and instability, then capitalise on these vulnerabilities. The poorer people are, the more insecure they are, the more they are exploited. Credit abuse and gambling are just two examples. There are many "opportunities" to capitalise on the vulnerable. Scarcity creates weakness, making it difficult for people to retain assets, which are often lost to the benefit of the rich (exploiter.) Consider how banks fleeced clients on overdraft fees. People, pushed into a corner and struggling, are exploited. This is the Vacuum Up effect, and it works well. It's the complete opposite of trickle down. Obviously, the wealthy one per cent have to hide this nasty practice from the majority, so they dressed it up in sheep's clothing and called it "trickle down" - our benefactor. They carried on lying about trickle down while fully aware the opposite was working in their favour.

"There are two ways of invading private property; the first, by which the poor plunder the rich... sudden and violent; the second, by which the rich plunder the poor, slow and legal."

An Inquiry into the Principles and Policy of the Government of the United States (1814) by John Taylor,

Summary.

We will always have a rich/poor divide. There is nothing wrong with it. It's only wrong when the divide becomes a chasm, with too much wealth held by a few.

The notion that it's good for all if the rich get richer is a total fallacy. It's only good if all get richer proportionately. Skewed wealth distribution in favour of the rich is harmful to the majority. The greater the divide, the greater the harm felt by the majority - it's that simple.

The most effective and practical way to ensure fair wealth/value distribution is through implementing a new measurement standard which will ensure fair and balanced distribution at the source of its creation.

This will go a long way in ensuring fairer wealth distribution, thereby limiting the negative consequences of skewed wealth distribution. However, there are other unfair practices within the rentier economy which inhibit economic growth to the disadvantage of the majority. These protectionist laws, implemented to protect the rich, which do not serve the majority, need reversing. We also need greater regulation to protect the economically vulnerable.

Chapter 4
Create a true investment culture.

The big picture I've painted so far shows how the rich have used an inadequate and inappropriate measurement standard to optimise profits for themselves. They then manipulate the system to free markets from regulations so they can generate even greater profits. All this accumulated wealth does not trickle down as the hoax proclaimed it would. Instead, it's used to leverage further wealth opportunities, using the vacuum-up effect, and to invest in the rentier economy. This increases their wealth even further. However, there still remains another realm which they have manipulated to their benefit - that's the investment market. The investment market has been manipulated to serve the rich one per cent at the expense of the majority. That's what we look at in this chapter.

Most of us understand the term "invest" to mean, among other things, a commitment to the long haul. We invest time, money or both in our education and careers because we know that over time the rewards justify the investment. Therefore, it might be strange to learn that we need to call on the "investors" in our economy to return to the basics of investing. For them to understand the businesses they are investing in, to believe in them, and to invest in them over the long haul, sticking with them through good and bad times. To stop their short-term commodity trading, which does not serve the economy well.

Shares are nothing more than commodities to them, where the name of the game is to "buy and sell" and make as much profit from these transactions as possible. They are not investors as investment requires thought, understanding, and a willingness to persevere through thick and thin in pursuit of long-term objectives. Trading is about buying low and selling high and doing it as often as possible. To this end, stockbrokers have developed sophisticated algorithms and have super fast computers do the trades for them based on share trading trends. It has nothing to do with the principles of investment whatsoever.

Just think what a massive screw-up this is, where the fundamentals of investment are not followed and where the so-called "owners" of business are no more than transient holders of share certificates, interested only in short-term profits and dividends. A system which couldn't care less about the long-term prospects of the business and it's stakeholders, most of whom have substantially more "invested" in the business than its share certificate holders.

This system serves a small, elite group of investors and their stockbrokers. The whole system is a complete screw-up unless of course, you are an investor or stockbroker playing the system. For the rest of us, and the economy, it's a screw-up.

Traders, not investors.
Let's face it - despite the illusion created by stockbrokers, where you see offices filled with rows of computers and brightly-coloured charts and graphs adorned across their screens, there is very little "investment" going on. All this paraphernalia and their systems are there to support trading, nothing else. They have software using super-fast computers which trade with other computers using sophisticated algorithms based on trading data. They transact billions in minutes, without human intervention. The system analyses trading data and predicts future prices. Based on this alone the system decides to buy or sell. None of the decisions are based on any understanding of the business's underlying ability to create long-term value, the most fundamental investment criteria of all. It's about trading, not investing. Shares are a commodity which they trade in. It's about making small percentage gains on massive amounts of transactions; nothing to do with investment whatsoever. Trading, rather than investing, does not help grow the economy, it hinders it. The two major reasons for this are, it creates market instability and produces poor long term growth. Trading also ensures there is no long-term commitment, or drive, by shareholders for the prosperity of their investment. Trading represents an easy and relatively safe profit venture. Investment, on the other hand, involves long-term commitment and therefore risk, as the future is always uncertain. However, long-term investments generally provide far greater returns. Effort and commitment are eventually

rewarded. You will see this contrast between trading and investing throughout this chapter. Trading represents "take what you can now, don't worry about the future" and investment of "commitment and hard work to grow something worthwhile."

I know investors and stockbrokers will deny their current practices are hurting the economy and are thus an area for concern. Of course, they would, they don't want their practices exposed, as armed with the facts, people will demand change. They will demand that changes be made which serve the wider community rather than a select few.

Consider the following in support of the argument that the investment community has a vested interest in maintaining their short-term, manipulative trading practices. Financial capital which is traded freely in an open market is highly volatile, moving quickly and frequently to achieve the best returns. Fortunes can be made through only minor shifts in share prices, which investors are continually looking for, or creating. Rumours, heard first, present an ideal profit opportunity. For example, a rumour heard of a major R & D (Research & Development) investment becomes an ideal opportunity for a broker to profit. He buys on this rumour. The R & D announcement sets off the upward movement of the share price at which point the broker sells out, having made a fortune. Buy low, sell high, and do it often - that's the name of the game. Brokers are looking for market "blips" which will drive prices up or down as these price variations are how they profit. Market instability is a crucial ingredient in their profit plan. Rumours, quarterly results, trading announcements, dividend announcements, and other market activities; all short-term, insignificant events, when compared to the business's long-term prospects. These market "blips" allow brokers to profit, and ownership to change like the wind. These minor market activities have little or no influence on true investors, who are in it for the long haul.

Some may argue that these investors are not myopic and are not driven by quarterly earnings, rumours or other market "blips." It is difficult to accept this hypothesis, for if their logic were correct, then in the above scenario, there would have been hectic buy-in after the R & D announcement and after that limited trade as the investors held onto their shares, waiting for the fruits of the R & D investment to pay off. This isn't the reality of the situation at all. A poorly traded share is currently seen as unattractive. How can this be true if investors are in it for the long haul? Further "evidence" that many investors are myopic lies in the fact that they rely on quarterly earnings for evaluation purposes, which shows just how short-termed and narrowly focused they are. If their evaluation tools are trading data and quarterly financial results, how can they be anything else but short-termed and narrowly focused? Market volatility, driven by short-term events (such as rumour and quarterly earnings - "blips") provides the ideal trading environment for astute brokers to profit from.

Back to basics.

We have to go back to basics, where business owners become owners in the true sense. Where they believe in and are committed to its long-term future: people prepared to stick with their investment when things get tough; not transient holders of share certificates who can divest themselves in a blink of an eye. True owners take great care and responsibility for the well-being of the many facets of their business's long-term prospects. However, in their absence, this care and responsibility is shifted onto "proxy owners" - professional managers. Unfortunately, these managers don't have the long-term interests of the business at heart (just as their owner's don't) Their objective is to optimise short-term profits and maximise dividend payouts, as that's what their transient owners want and reward them for. The consequences of this are, managers denude the business of its underlying value to generate profit. It's easy to make a profit while stripping value. Most people will be unaware that managers are "robbing Peter to pay Paul." If they are, or suspect managers of it, it doesn't concern them as they aren't interested in the long-term either.

As there is no correlation between financial profit and value creation, managers can mask their value stripping activities behind strong profit results. We all know it's possible to make a financial profit yet destroy value, and we also know it's possible to create underlying value yet show a financial loss. Financial profit masks value creation activities, yet it is these value creation activities which build underlying business value which supports and sustains future profit. So while it's important that we measure financial performance, it's equally important that we measure value creation activities, unless we want to be "led up the garden path" by our financials. Without the two, we are "flying blind." Financial and value creation measures are as different as chalk and cheese. One deals in pounds and pence and the other in probabilities and relationships. Financial measures are exclusive, short-term orientated and backwards-looking, whereas value creation measures are fully inclusive, long-term and forward-looking. Therefore, you cannot use a single model (e.g. the Accounting Model) and hope to get an accurate picture of business's true performance; you need a fully integrated value creation model based on the causal nature of business. Our primary focus must be on the value creation processes - the true profit driver!

As managers are evaluated against their financial performance, they are discouraged from investing in long-term wealth creating opportunities, because the more they invest in long-term value creators, the lower the book value of the business in the short-term.

Outlays on R & D represent investments in potential new income streams, which should generate revenue well into the future. However, our financial measures treat them as worthless by expensing them. In effect, it takes the R & D asset and discards it. R & D is an asset as it enables the creation of income (i.e. it has value). The more you invest in R & D, the less profitable your business appears. The same applies to marketing costs invested to establish brands, enter new markets, or gain market share. All these outlays are investments to acquire new customers who should generate revenue well into the future, yet our financial measures expenses these outlays, reducing the business's profit. Therefore, managers are encouraged to cut back on potentially profitable marketing programmes and R & D to make sure quarterly earnings look good!

The short-term tenure of senior managers encourages some of them to cut costs "below the bone" and to shun medium to long-term investment opportunities to further their own objectives. In some instances, figures are even manipulated to "improve earnings." The extent of this practice is unknown, yet it is believed to be prevalent.

Predatory management
driven by excessive remuneration.

Manages are becoming more predatory in pursuit of profits because transient owners are paying them ridiculous remuneration packages as their proxy owners. In return, they expect them to deliver good profits and dividends.

Transient owners don't care what's paid to managers, as long as they deliver profits and dividends. Managers remuneration, to them, is "small potatoes" in relation to the bigger profit picture. "To get the best, you must pay market rates" is the mantra quoted. This pushes up market rates for executives. It's counter productive and of course a load of baloney to believe they are worth it, as I will explain. However, managers make sure they do everything to optimise profits and dividends, thereby ensuring they are "the best" and in line for unjustifiably high remuneration deals.

Things are bad enough when you consider that our business measurement standard fosters a profiteering approach. However, when investors introduce additional poor practices through unjustifiably high remuneration packages for executives, to ruthlessly drive profits (mainly through value stripping), can things get any worse?

Most businesses agree and support the concept of participative management, which has enabled businesses to flatten management hierarchies and operate more efficiently and effectively. It works because it involves everybody in the decision-making process. Big businesses which are run by proxy owners use and promote participative management. Therefore, how can shareholders justify remuneration packages for their top brass which are so much higher than those of their minions, when clearly decisions are the result of a participative process. Obviously, the final decision is made by the head, but its usually a rubber stamping of a process involving collective thought and decisions, not the genius of an individual. Today, individuals make less of an impact than in the past when non-participative structures and processes prevailed. This is not to negate the role of leadership. It's still important, and justifies fair and reasonable reward, but not absurdly distorted packages. This must have their minions questioning their worth, wondering why they are so under-valued in relation to their bosses, whom they know are not superheroes. As a consequence, productivity plummets. As explained in the previous chapter, when somebody takes a slice of the pie greater than their contribution, that represents rent (or profiteering.) It's counterproductive and leads to distrust. Huge salaries and bonuses cannot be ascribed to the contribution of a single person. Team work is critical to a business's success. When disproportionately large incentive scheme are introduced for the CEO and other executives, this breaks down teamwork, as it breaks all the rules of fairness. When banks pay their executive's obscene packages and the average person struggles to service their debts due to excessively high interest rates, they become resentful. It all adds fuel to the fire of how unfair our economy is. Very few people believe their CEO should earn what they earn in a year, in just three days. People accept they should earn a good salary, but good and obscene are worlds apart.

Are investors and stockbrokers fully to blame?
Are investors and shareholders to blame for the fact that we have lost our way and no longer adhere to the sound principles of good investment? No, not entirely. One can understand how the situation has degenerated into this state. After all, traders have no comprehensive information upon which to base their decisions about long-term business performance. Their only source of information is trading data and short-term financial records - hardly enough to make informed decisions about future performance. Consequently, as they cannot make informed investment decisions, they are forced to trade. As a result, they have developed extremely sophisticated commodity trading techniques, but commodity trading rather than long-term investment only benefits this elite group. Why should they want

change? They have adapted the system to work for themselves. Only when we provide them with a fully inclusive business measurement standard which will help them accurately assess the long-term value creation potential of business, can they become investors. You cannot expect investors to invest if they are not given the right information to make informed decisions. This is the first step in solving this problem.

Obviously, as intelligent people, they appreciate this as much as you and I, but they have done nothing to call for change. Why should they - they are doing well for themselves using the current systems.

Investing for the long-term.
Getting investors to invest over the long-term offers many benefits. Market stability is one of the key benefits. If Investors cannot divest at the drop of a hat, they have as much, or more, invested in the business than other stakeholders and will fight to protect those interest for the benefit of all stakeholders. Currently, they will cut and run and leave the business and its stakeholders, who often have a considerable investment in the business, to suffer the consequences. Often businesses are weakened by value stripping over extended periods by transient owners and their proxy owners, leaving the business weak and vulnerable. By ensuring investors are "locked in" over the long-term, they take greater care of underlying value creators, so they are not left vulnerable at some future date. When investors act as genuine owners, they ensure all facets of the business are managed effectively. They don't employ managers to strip value to bolster profits and thus pay unearned dividends. They don't pay managers excessive salaries for these destructive processes. They don't pay managers to weaken the long-term survival of the business. Long-term owners become more demanding of managers, ensuring all facets of the business are managed effectively, not just financial matters. Financial matters only represent a small percentage of the value creation potential of business. Investors are not swayed from wise long-term strategies in favour of short-term market "blips" which can see multiple millions wiped from the business's share capital in the blink of an eye.

More regulation is required.

While providing a balanced measurement standard is key to addressing the problem of long-term investment, it won't be the only solution required. We will need to regulate investment to prohibit short and medium term trading. This will force investors into making informed decisions by becoming true owners where they will hold managers accountable for all facets of stakeholder management as key to sustained long-term profit. They will become more demanding and involved, as owners should be because their investment is at risk. They cannot easily divest, so they take effective control to drive long-term value creation for all. It will end the ridiculous remuneration of managers as demands on resources will increase and costs will need to be cut on non-productive expenditure. As long-term owners, they will appreciate that these grotesquely distorted remuneration packages represent non-productive expenditure (rent). If not cut, owners rewards will be affected, and they will do everything to ensure this does not happen.

Investors and stockbrokers will squeal like fat pigs and resist these measures as their easy and relatively risk-free access to huge profits will be over as we return to the basics of investment. They may squeal as much as they like, but current practices only serve to enrich them, not the wider community. They have used the system for their benefit for far too long. Time for change.

Summary.

Business owners must act like owners, where the long-term interests of the business are their concern. Where they realise that long-term success is achieved through the astute management of the value creation interests of all stakeholders, not just their own.

The current situation, where "owners" are no more than transient share certificate holders only interested in trading their certificates for a short-term profit, with no long-term interest or commitments to the business, set in motion serious undesirable events. These undesirable events are detrimental to society and economy.

As current owners are transient, they appoint proxy owners - professional managers to run the business. These managers are only interested in delivering short-term profits and maximum dividends, as that is what their owners demand. Much of the "profit" generated is made by harsh profiteering from staff and suppliers by holding down salary increases and extending supplier terms. They create further profit by stripping value and/or under investing in value generators. Dividends paid are therefore unearned, and this weakens the business over the long-term. Shareholders pay excessive executive salaries to achieve these results, which drives value denuding practices even further and harder, doing even greater damage. Business longevity and other stakeholder interests are put at high risk. Often, stakeholders have more "invested" in a business than their transient "owners" do - the people who don't care about the business's long-term prospects as they can quickly and easily divest, with little or no harm to themselves.

To stop all this, we need to provide better investment tools in the form of a new business measurement standard. A standard which will provide greater insight into the value creation potential of business over the medium and long-term. We also need to improve regulations to stop short-term trading, to slow the flow of money down and provide the market greater stability.

Chapter 5
Rein in rampant consumerism - act collectively.

In the four proceeding chapters I dealt with the major factors which cause inequality; business measures, free markets, the rentier economy and the investment market. As important as these problems are in addressing economic injustice, they are secondary concerns when compared to the protection of our environment. We are facing the ecological collapse of our planet with devastating consequences. Our future depends upon a healthy and supportive environment capable of supporting all life, not just ours. The stark reality is - we cannot continue as before and sustain current levels of consumption, waste, pollution and environmental degradation and achieve this. We have to change. This chapter is about that change.

Rampant consumerism - another cover-up.
The wealthy one per cent drive rampant consumption as it adds to their wealth. However, they don't concern themselves with its consequences, as that lies within the domain of "the common good." This does not concern them. Their only concern is to make a profit, and not to be "caught with blood on their hands" (i.e. not to be found responsible for any adverse environmental/social consequences.) To this end, they concoct messages which encourage rampant consumerism, while telling us not to worry about the consequences, as they are taken care of. They relentlessly feed society with these messages and cover up the consequences as best they can, until the person-in-the-street believes it as the truth.

We've all heard of the BOGOF (Buy One Get One Free) offer. All part of the extensive arsenal used by business to get us to buy more. As consumers, we are bombarded by offers of this type, until it enters our psyche. We believe it's reasonable and acceptable to consume without regard to its consequences. That's precisely what vested interests want you to believe and be comfortable with.

The harsh reality is - global resources cannot sustain ever-increasing consumer demands. The situation is made worse as emerging economies try to emulate those of developed economies. Unless we as consumers accept responsibility for our consumption and appreciate that we have to live within our sustainable means, this will develop into the biggest screw-up of all!

Vested interests continue to promote a message of opulence and waste. If you can afford it - buy it. Even if you can't afford it - buy it, as we will lend you the money. It doesn't matter if you over-consume, you have a right to - you have earned it. Waste doesn't matter (we can manage it.) Indulge yourself, it's your right, which you have earned.

The facts are - nobody has a right to cause irreparable harm to our environment or consume in an unsustainable way, irrespective of who they are, or whom they think they are. You cannot earn this right under any circumstances, and never will. You may have worked hard all your life and in your retirement believe you have "earned the right" to flit around the globe leaving your huge ugly carbon footprint everywhere. Sorry – but you haven't earned that right and never will, no matter who you are, or how hard you've worked. We have all been loaned this beautiful planet to use for a short time; not to abuse it so others may not enjoy the same benefits. Our excessive consumption, pollution and waste have to be brought under control - we have no choice. Our disposable, throwaway economy may be convenient and time-saving, but it's unsustainable, wasteful and polluting.

Some say there are economies to our disposable, throwaway economy, and they are correct - false economies! We save a little time now but pay a huge future price. Often manufacturers and consumers are not affected by the long-term consequences of their consumption, which others have to bare. Unfortunately, eventually we all have to pay, and the price is far higher than the short-term benefits gained at the time.

Vested interest's short-term sales and profit obsession drives rampant consumerism, which they will do anything to increase. They are not concerned with the negative medium/long-term consequences of their products consumption. Consumers ignore the problems as well because it's often hidden from them and they are made to believe it's not their problem, as this would reduce sales and profits.

To understand the implications of rampant consumerism, I'm going to explain the background to the problem in a little more detail. However, before I do that I need to be clear on the meaning of "rampant consumerism", as I have seen some economists defend it. In January 2015 John Sentamu, Archbishop of York and Justin Welby, Archbishop of Canterbury lashed out at rampant consumerism. An economist called Ryan Bourne published an article in the Telegraph on 16th January 2015 to defend rampant consumerism. Mr Bourne points out to the two Archbishops that our standard-of-living has improved dramatically over the past four decades, so they should not complain. Unfortunately for Mr Bourne, he's a victim of the misinformation spread by vested interests, or otherwise, he's playing his part in trying to spread it further. Both Archbishops were trying to point out that rampant consumerism is adversely affecting our quality-of-life, which is true. Mr Bourne was highlighting our improved standard-of-living, which is something entirely different. However, as vested interests have conflated the two terms (as explained in chapter one), you can see why poor Mr Bourne himself is confused. (Please also refer to Appendix A on this matter.)

It is the extent to which vested interest encourages consumption and hides the consequences which is the problem. Consumption is out of control. We pollute, produce unmanageable amounts of waste, and live beyond sustainable levels. This rampant consumerism is driven by the insidious message (which I introduced earlier,) and promoted by vested interests to help drive sales and profits, irrespective of the long-term costs to others. The message is that it's okay to consume as much as you like because you've worked hard and you deserve it. Don't worry about waste, pollution and sustainability, we've got that covered. They haven't, they simply hide problems, until they become too big to hide any more. Plastics polluting the ocean is a case in point. It's just one of the hundreds of examples.

What I've said so far is nothing new, we are all aware of these problems. Perhaps not the extent to which vested interests have manipulated the message and hidden the truth, but that's what they are good at. Not fake news, but fake messages. I'm now going to provide a broader understanding of our need to rein in rampant consumerism, and it involves us, as consumers taking more responsibilities. Yes, we have been manipulated and lied to, but that does not hide the fact that we bare some responsibility for the environmental mess we are in. It's not all about the fault of others.

Inclusive Theory.

The issue of whom business should create wealth/value for is central to our society and economy. What we do in business is critically important because it operates at a micro, or cellular level. It provides the DNA of our society and economy. Our understanding of whom business should create value for has evolved and continues to evolve.

It started with the idea that shareholders should be the beneficiaries as they provide the financial capital and take the financial risk. This made sense. However, over time concerns grew. Marketers suggested that "customer value" was important. They argued that if we do not continually increase customer value, they will go elsewhere. This also made sense. "What about employees?" argued Human-Resource experts, "they too will go elsewhere unless looked after." "What about the environment?" conjectured environmentalists. "If we continue to destroy what supports us, we have no future." They to make a good case. And so the legitimate claims to become beneficiaries of value creation grew. All claimants make a plausible and logical case for their fair share.

The facts are, there are many participants, or stakeholders involved in the activities of business, such as, customers, staff, suppliers, the community in which the business trades, the environment, as well as shareholders. If all these participants are not "looked after" their support, in the future, may be difficult to achieve. This will make future value creation for the business owners, or shareholders, more difficult. Consequently, sustained, long-term value creation is about creating value for all participants involved in the activities of business, not just one, or a group of select participants.

It's not an altruistic, or "airy fairy" social belief to suggest that all participants be rewarded fairly, but rather a common-sense approach. Adopting a short-term, profiteering mentality, of rewarding one participant at the expense of others, creates an unsustainable imbalance in our economy. When value is more evenly spread among all participants, we have a stronger economy, which leads to a brighter future for all, not just select participants.

For business to be successful, it has to create value for all its participants. You have to see business from a balanced perspective. If you only see shareholder value creation as your sole objective, then you will never achieve it as shareholder value creation is inextricably linked with all other participants. Unless you create value for all participants, long-term shareholder value creation is a wild, unattainable dream.

As obvious as this may appear, we have not yet made the transition to "Stakeholder Theory" (as proposed by Edward Freeman,) away from "Shareholder Value Theory" (attributed to Milton Friedman,) which suggests the interests of shareholders be placed above all others. The reason we can't make the transition is a simple one. Our economy relies on comparable measures, so unless we can measure stakeholder value creation on a universally comparable basis, businesses will not make the transition. Instead, they will continue to rely on universally applicable financial measures. While not ideal, it is argued that some comparison is better than none. Unfortunately, the use of our financial measures as a business measure has led to undesirable consequences, resulting in it becoming the root cause of our most serious social, environmental, economic and business problems. Therefore, we need to adopt the more balanced approach of "Stakeholder Theory," but this is dependent upon developing a universally applicable value creation measurement framework, which, until now, has been unavailable.

Until we develop and introduce a new business measurement standard, which will provide a balanced approach, and protect the interests of all stakeholders, we hurtle towards the destruction of our socioeconomic and environmental systems, as we know it. Because of the scale and speed of destruction, I believe "Stakeholder Theory" does not go far enough in providing a solution, hence the introduction of "Inclusive Theory", my small "tweak" on "Stakeholder Theory."

The backdrop to this theory are reports like those produced by the WWF and SustainAbility, (plus many others) who conclude that "the Earth cannot keep up with the demand our economy is placing on its ecological assets. Evidence is mounting that the sheer volume of resources flowing through the global economy has become today's key environmental challenge and as human demand for resources grows the Earth's life-supporting natural capital will be liquidated at ever-increasing rates."

If we are to address these problems there has to be a new understanding within business (i.e. the introduction of a new balanced measurement standard,) and between society, if we have any chance of averting disaster. Basically, we need a new social contract between business and society. Business has to function as a societal tool. It can no longer be a self-serving mechanism for shareholder enrichment at the expense of others, but rather a tool to serve all stakeholders. Critically, shareholders still need to be rewarded, (this being the primary concern of business) but not at the expense of other stakeholders. Consequently, Capitalism, or the spirit of free enterprise, remains the ideal mechanism to deliver growth and upliftment, provided it is based on balanced rewards for all stakeholders. Currently, this is not the case. This is not the fault of Capitalism. The problem lies with our inadequate and inappropriate business measurement standard, where we use financial measures as a business measure, thereby placing a financial bias on everything, favouring the fortunes of shareholders over all others.

In a new understanding between business and society, we must all accept responsibility and accountability. It's not somebody else's problem, or a case of, "I don't care," because, the outcomes impact us all. Consequently, it's not just about business doing its bit but also about the critical role consumers and society play in business. For example, our new measurement standard will hold business accountable for upstream environmental/social impacts (i.e. the business fully inherits the environmental/social impacts of its suppliers.) It is also responsible for their own processing and downstream environmental/social impacts. Downstream refers to the impact your product/service has on customers/consumers who use what you produce. So, if for example, you are a brewery, then you must accept some responsibility for the social consequences of alcohol consumption. You would be required to pay higher business taxes to fund your impacts. Why should other businesses, who have no adverse social impact have to fund the consequences your product potentially generates. Therefore, it is only fair that the consumer picks up the upstream environmental/social impacts of the products and services they consume. If business is vilified and driven out of business because of their overall poor environmental/social impact, then so too must the consumer be vilified and dissuaded from using products and services with a poor environmental and social/community impact. Consumers are as much part of the supply chain as any business, and must, therefore, be educated into accepting the responsibility for their purchases and their impacts.

"As long as there is a demand, business will fulfil it" is a mindset we can no longer tolerate. There are consequences to this and those producing and consuming while destroying or placing resources under undue stress, must be stopped, or face the consequences. The lifestyle enjoyed by most in the first world, and to which all others aspire are simply unaffordable in terms of natural resources. We as consumers have to take responsibility for these unsustainable consumption patterns. We have to review our consumption patterns and expectations in light of a growing population and our demands on limited and sometimes irreplaceable resources. What we demand and expect have to be tempered with these constraints. As consumers, it's our demands and expectations, which drive business, so we have a very important role to play on issues we are quite happy to blame on business. We blame them for exploiting scarce resources, pollution, cutting down rainforests and planting commercial products in their place, but we still demand the products responsible for this. We are the ones who set up the demand which results in unethical and unsustainable practice because as long as there's a demand, somebody will try to meet it. Our role is to temper our demands and expectations and become savvier in identifying wasteful, unsustainable, polluting and unethically sourced products. Products with a negative environmental and community impact need to be socially ostracised. We can't continue the way we are now; the responsibility for change lies with consumers as much as it does with business. As a society, rather than celebrate opulence, extravagance and waste, we have to learn to celebrate frugalness and, product longevity. This may not sound attractive, but I know our inventiveness will come up with enticing solutions.

"We are all in it together" sums up "Inclusive Theory." It's a small but important tweak to "Stakeholder Theory." We cannot expect a fundamental change that does not involve the most critical component of all - the consumer. Consumers ultimately determine demand. Therefore, they need to set their expectations in accordance with realities - no unbridled expectations just because they have the wherewithal. Consumers must take responsibility for their consumption and not attempt to pass it back upstream. It's not the large corporations chopping down forests to replace them with palm oil plants, or huge beef herds, but rather the consumer because the consumer creates the demand. Consumers must temper their demands based on all the good principles we expect business to uphold.

Consumers also have wider responsibilities to ensure all businesses (even those they have no relationship with) act responsibly, thereby ensuring we all keep a watchful eye over the most important social asset of all - business. We are all accountable and responsible.

Inclusive Theory differs from that of Stakeholder Theory in one important way. Stakeholder Theory says "reward all stakeholders appropriately". It sees the issue from a business perspective whereas Inclusive Theory sees the issue from a wider social perspective by including consumers in our collective responsibility. It says consumers are critical in the process as they establish demand and must, therefore, take far greater responsibility for their actions. It's not just about business actions – we are all in it together, and collectively, we must accept responsibilities for our actions. We serve our self-interest by adopting a community approach.

Taking responsibility.

The above represents the background to rampant consumerism. Key factors in addressing it lie in introducing a new, balanced measurement standard, which looks after the interests of all stakeholders. Secondly, vested interests need to play a major role in changing the message they currently promote. Rather than celebrate opulence and waste, we need to re-educate people to celebrate frugalness, product longevity and be resource conscious. The current message of opulence and waste permeates every facet of life. After all, it's the message vested interests have been so keen to promote over the decades. "Consume as much as you like and don't worry about the consequences, that's all taken care of." As an example of this take popular TV programmes which still promote the entirely wrong message. As an example of this wasteful and OTT (Over The Top) behaviour, consider the BBC TV programme called "Master Chef." It's a programme which encourages opulent waste of resources to serve the palate of the well-to-do, commonly referred to as "fine dining." As a national programme, it should encourage taking simple, inexpensive, sustainable foods to produce exceptional meals within an affordable budget. The winners should be those who produce the best from the least, not those who may make great tasting meals but at great cost and waste. Poorer nations, such as India, Mexico, Thailand (and others) have proved that taking simple, readily available ingredients can produce delicious meals. This food example applies to all facets of life. We, as consumers, need to cut back and learn to live a more minimalistic lifestyle. A sustainable lifestyle.

The message of frugalness, product longevity and resource-conscious consumption have to permeate every facet of life to support a sustainable, high quality-of-life for all, not just a select few. Our current mentality and behaviour is the antithesis of this. As a society, rather than celebrate opulence, extravagance and waste, we have to learn to celebrate frugalness and product longevity. Consumers, although bombarded and influenced by the wrong messages for decades, driving unsustainable consumption, have to take responsibility for their consumption and its consequences, as much as business has to. That's the principle of "Inclusive Theory."

We have got to start by disrupting vested interest's message of opulence, entitlement and disposability, to one of durability and sustainability. Studies have shown that people will abstain from individually beneficial but socially/environmentally harmful acts if they perceive most others do the same. That's the message we have to get the large media corporations to promote, but then they are in the pockets of the wealthy one per cent. The fall-back option is to regulate them - force them to support this message. Still, that's another battle, but we have the power, we are the ninety-nine per cent.

Summary.

We cannot continue consuming, wasting and polluting as we are now. We have to live in a more frugal, resource and waste conscious way.

A new business measurement standard will hold business accountable for their upstream (supplier), as well as downstream (consumer/user) impacts. In other words, the impact their production processes and use of their products have on the environment and society. However, we must go further and include consumers in the management of resources. Inclusive Theory promotes the inclusion of consumers in a new social contract with business, where we all become responsible for our actions.

It's up to business and government to promote Inclusive Theory, which will bring to an end the falsehoods business has promoted for decades that we can consume as much as we like because we deserve it, and not to worry about issues of sustainability, waste or pollution, as we can manage all of it. We can't.

The new message will be to celebrate frugalness, product longevity, resource and waste conscious consumption. We must live within our sustainable means, and nobody has the right to cause environmental damage through excessive pollution, consumption or any other reason. You are responsible for what you do; you cannot expect others to pick up the problems you create.

Chapter 6
Increase government involvement.

Vested interests would like us to believe that big governments are inefficient and an unreasonable burden on society, particularly the rich, through high taxation. This, in turn, limits their ability to invest and develop the economy, which impacts negatively on all – so we must resist big governments.

Logic does not support this reasoning, neither does the evidence. You've read how they make the money, keep it, or spend it in the rentier economy - either way we lose. It's just the narrative used to hide the truth. We learnt in Chapter Two how vested interests benefit by having small governments, and how this hurts the majority. For business, small government means less government intervention or free markets. It means they can do what they like – no interference. As Chapter Three shows, they then use their wealth to capitalise on the weakest and most vulnerable. Small governments are also less efficient in clamping down on tax avoidance and evasion, which is another advantage for them. Free markets and globalisation help weaken the negotiating strength of governments. Small government is held ransom to their demands. Often, this involves lowering taxes on corporates and wealthy, and increasing corporate welfare. However, the most important advantage of all is that small government isn't as expensive as big government; the wealthy one per cent's tax bill is considerably smaller. All these things benefit the wealthy, not the average citizen – it hurts them.

However, there is another reason they call for small governments, and that is to get government to outsource contracts, or divest themselves in providing certain services, which Big Business can then provide. This opens huge, profitable markets for them. This, they claim, leads to "lean governments", which are more efficient, as business is better at running commercial ventures.

Big government is a necessity.
The call for "lean", or small government, is driven by vested interest's needs, not those of the government or its citizens. The

purpose of government is to ensure the highest possible standard-of-living and quality-of-life for its citizens, while protecting the environment. There are many services the government must provide to achieve this, which cost money - lots of it. Therefore, the responsibilities of government make big governments a necessity, which we cannot escape. For the many services a government must provide, it can run them themselves, outsource them, or divest and have business run them. A further alternative is not to provide them at all. Whatever option is adopted, there is a cost associated with it. Outsourcing is a means of shifting costs away from the government. Divesting is a means of hiding costs. Using either method is just playing the accounting game, of moving costs around. It creates the illusion of having a leaner government, but these services are still provided and paid for. Of course, a government may opt not to provide their citizens with the services which more progressive governments do. However, let us not forget that their citizens bear the costs of not having these services. In other words, they lower their citizens quality-of-life to the extent of not providing these services enjoyed by citizens in other countries. Their quality-of-life drops in proportion to the cost they must now bear. So, whether a government provides the service in-house, outsources it, divest itself of the service or does not provide the service, there is a cost associated, and it's large.

So, big government is a necessity no matter which way we look at it. However, for those who believe the nonsense fed them by vested interests and believe that lean governments are a measure of an efficient government, then they are in for a nasty surprise. One can shift and hide costs with relative ease making it appear that one has a lean government. However, cost shifting, hiding and cutting, places quality-of-life at risk, as cost manipulation becomes the objective, not the provision of quality services. The objective of government is to provide its citizens with the highest standard-of-living and quality-of-life, so they should focus on that, and stop trying to shift or hide the costs merely to mislead us.

This does leave us with the question which Big Business would like you to believe that, "Business is better at running services than government. We can modernise and run these services more efficiently, all for a reasonable cost, with no unpleasant cost surprises. This helps cut the size of government and all its wasteful bureaucracy." Is this true or is it just more misleading nonsense to make them rich? Let's have a look at these options now.

Outsourcing.

Outsourcing sounds enticing. Greater efficiencies, modernisation and cost containment, with no unpleasant cost surprises, at current costs or less. The reality is entirely different. In an open and buoyant labour market, labour cost reduction requires corner cutting. They pay staff less and/or provide fewer or poorer benefits. Opportunities to modernise are available to government and business in equal measure. Unexpected and high unforeseen costs, are never "contained", but passed on in subsequent price increases. Big Business needs to make a profit out of these services. Efficiencies may account for their profits, as government departments not exposed to the rigours of competitive markets, can become less efficient over time. Departmental inefficiencies are a problem, but they are also an opportunity. It's an opportunity for government to find and realise efficiencies. Government employees owe it to their fellow citizens to root out waste and inefficiencies.

In the long-term, the benefits of outsourcing are marginal if at all. They help make the financials look good, by shifting costs off government balance sheets. If Governments don't outsource and go on efficiency drives, there are real opportunities to reduce costs, without compromising service quality. The favoured option is to keep it in-house and look for efficiencies.

Divesting.

In the next section on "Becoming more involved", I recommend the benefits of greater government involvement, and identify types of businesses they should become more involved in. In the past, when sense prevailed, these were the businesses governments ran, for strategic reasons and/or protecting key industries. However, today, free markets and globalisation brainwashing, together with extensive lobbying by vested interests have changed government's attitude.

The same logic which applied to outsourcing applies to divesting. In the long-term there are no cost savings, with a high probability of a decline in quality, because of conflicting objectives business faces - profit versus quality. As shareholder interests are paramount, decisions taken behind closed doors are in favour of profit. The reality is, a rent-seeking objective underlie decisions to become involved in privatisation (i.e. taking over services previously run by the government.) Again, divesting, like outsourcing deprives governments the opportunity to gain efficiencies and thus reduce costs without compromising quality of service. Consequently, divesting makes little or no long-term sense. It cannot be the preferred option.

Reduce or provide no services.
The role of government is to provide its citizens with the highest standard-of-living and quality-of-life possible. The more services it provides, the higher its citizens quality-of-life. The fewer services it provides, the lower their quality-of-life. One would think that if government does not provide a particular service, or reduces the extent of the service, it would save costs? That's true, it saves direct costs, however, in so doing, it incurs an opportunity cost. An opportunity cost is the cost of losing the advantages/benefits they would have received had they spent the money, but now have to forgo. As an example, central government in the UK is cutting funding it provides local councils. As a result, local councils are cutting services they provide, such as closing libraries. Local citizens now have to fund reading material themselves or forgo the pleasure of reading. This lowers their quality-of-life. The opportunity cost incurred by government and local government is a less educated and contented population, which could adversely affect their productivity and health. These can have long lasting effects which could well exceed the cost of short-term cost savings.

So, Big government is a reality. The other reality is that shifting these costs via outsourcing or divesting, does not improve quality of services over the long-term. What it does is remove the opportunity for government to reduce costs through the introduction of efficiencies, without compromising the quality of service. Non-provision of services is a cost borne by its citizens, so a high degree of non-provision impoverishes its citizens. This means the government has failed to meet its obligations to its citizens, which is to serve and protect them.

So, there is no truth to the myth that small government is beneficial to society, to the contrary, it's highly detrimental. Only vested interests benefit, and they don't care what harm is done through spreading this myth. There is just too much evidence out there which shows that big governments are socially and economically beneficial. They are also environmentally beneficial. When governments spend the money to research environmental impacts and solutions, as well as enforce regulations, we all benefit way beyond the investment.

Shifting priorities.
We must be clear, government's first priority is to its citizens, and then that of business. Obviously, business is critically important. It's the goose which lays the golden egg. We need to look after the goose. It's a delicate balance, where conflicting interests need to be reconciled. However, over the past four decades, the balance between citizens and business has gone out of kilter, where the golden goose no longer shares what she lays, yet we all toil to keep her alive. Governments are put under pressure by influential and powerful vested interests to shift their priority away from its citizens, onto the goose which they own. Governments lower taxes to support business, thereby lowering the quality-of-life of its citizens. They change laws to protect the goose at the cost of citizens well-being. In allowing this balance to shift in the wrong direction, governments fail their citizens - their first priority. If businesses were more socially and environmentally responsible, many of these problems would go away. A new measurement standard, which encourages these responsibilities would be most beneficial. Government's role in resolving conflicting interests would be minimised. However, there would still be many other areas where it needs to shift its priorities back in favour of citizens over business.

The case for government involvement.

There are creative and innovative people all around the world. Many live in developing economies with poor infrastructure and support. It is this lack of infrastructure and support which hinders them in bringing their products/services to the market. Most fail. Success or failure is primarily dependent on government investment. It provides the infrastructure, sets and enforces the rules. Society needs to work collectively to make the investments in "public goods" for all to benefit. Leaving such investments to the private sector will result in underinvestment as they are not interested in the common good. No one succeeds on one's own. We succeed because of the supportive infrastructure around us. The many smart, hardworking people living in developing economies will never make it and will remain poor because of a lack of supportive infrastructure. Physical and institutional infrastructure, developed through collective action over generations are the shoulders our economy rides on.

It must be appreciated that such investment must be maintained and preferably increased. The stronger our public sector, the stronger our society and economy. We need to invest in public goods such as R&D, infrastructure, education, social security nets, health, etc. This is what provides our society and economy with its strength - weaken them, and you weaken both. That's why free markets and globalisation are so wrong - they want this infrastructure weakened.

Becoming more involved.

Every chapter so far, and every subsequent chapter calls for greater government involvement. We need government to play a key role in introducing a new business measurement standard, and to stop and redress free markets. To halt and redress the growth of the rentier economy. To oversee new rules and regulations governing investment. To put an end to rampant consumerism and to help implement Inclusive Theory. In the first section of this chapter, I call for governments to stop outsourcing and divesting themselves of services, as long-term quality of service will decline with Big Business extracting ever bigger profits at the cost of quality of service. Government must not stop there. They should become more involved both directly and indirectly in running and supporting business development. Big government is a necessity.

Direct involvement.

Governments have a duty to protect their citizens interests, so that means government should run core services such as, big infrastructure businesses and key industrial/strategic industries which are marginally profitable. This is to protect and sustain them over the long-term, which business cannot guarantee. This provides a secure society and economy by knowing key infrastructure is protected. Any strategically important businesses and/or businesses central to supporting the quality-of-life, which if lost, could be a risk, and/or cause considerable disruption and time in replacing. Examples would be:-

Energy,

Transportation (Rail, Water, Road, Air),

Water,

Education (Primary/Secondary/Higher),

Health,

Housing (Primary),

Security,

Key industrial/strategic businesses which are marginally profitable, e.g. Steel manufacturing in the UK

Again, the list is not comprehensive, just sufficient to demonstrate the point.

Recently, I watched a TV programme where a local Scottish community erected four wind turbines which were connected to the national electricity grid. These four turbines earned the community £1 million per annum profit, which was ploughed back into community projects. A proposal for the erection of a further thirty six turbines in the area were called for by the local authority. The group who ran the four turbines put forward a proposal for other communities to become involved and to submit a joint proposal to erect and run them. They were competing against a large energy group who had proposed a 20% community stake in their proposal. This stake would pay the community £1 million per annum. The community project estimated that they could earn £10 million per annum for the community. The local authorities appeared to be favouring the energy company, saying local communities could not fund large scale endeavours such as this. This was strenuously denied by the community project leader. I am of the firm belief that if the government backed such a scheme, it would be a massive success. Rather than plough an additional £9 million per annum back into local communities this money will go to rich shareholders. To add insult to injury, the energy company is a large French company.

This example illustrates why governments should become more involved in business, particularly when it comes to core services such as the provision of energy. Business needs to extract profits, which could otherwise be used for the common good. I'm not suggesting that government take over all businesses, only those already identified. We need free enterprise, which is driven by the profit motive, to help improve both standard-of-living and quality-of-life. I think its a screw-up when capable and keen communities, run as non-profit organisations who plough their earnings back into community projects, which builds the fabric of society, lose projects to Big Business, so they can line their own pockets. What a disgrace!

Indirect involvement.
The second part of greater government involvement includes better support to develop and protect business. This includes amongst other things:-
Trade protection
Support / Incentives
R&D

Trade protection.
Vested interests vehemently tell us that protectionism is bad for our economy, as protected industries become uncompetitive and over time citizens have to pay a higher price for poorer quality. This is untrue and another instance of misleading information. As we have already learnt so far, vested interests want "free markets" so they can produce anywhere in the world (as cheaply as possible) and sell everywhere without limitations or restrictions (thereby optimising profits.) This is good for them but not national economies who lose jobs, lose revenue, have a poor balance of payments and have to pick up the social costs of

unemployment and other cuts imposed by a weaker economy. Vested interests get rich – super rich, but their wealth, unfairly accumulated (because of our use of an inadequate and inappropriate measurement standard) does not trickle down and benefit others. Much of these transnational's income escapes taxation in the countries it was earned. How can trade protection which tries to stop this from happening be bad for national economies? It isn't. Protectionism is a valuable tool in the government's arsenal. It has been used successfully in building strong economies for many years all around the globe. It has now become a "dirty" word used in hushed language by those who promote globalisation. We need to start thinking of globalisation as the dirty word, not protectionism.

Support and Incentives.
If a government does not run strategic/key businesses, it should provide greater support and incentives (when and where appropriate) to build a strong backbone for the economy. Protectionism, support and incentives are temporary measures, which need regular review to ensure they remain appropriate in serving the wider needs of government and the economy. They are not permanent measures but transient, implemented to protect the economy. They should be thought of as "medication for the economy" taken when ill, but not when well. There are instances where incentives have been in place for many years and perversely now serve the needs of the rich at the expense of everybody else. What was originally intended is no longer relevant, but the incentives/support remains. Obviously, this is bad and needs to be effectively regulated and reviewed. It's bad practice to have a patient become dependent on medication through overuse. The same applies to economic medication.

R&D (Research & Development.)
R&D plays a key part in the competitiveness of most industries. For some industries the government should play a role in shouldering some of these costs. The more a government underwrites R&D the more it can give its industries a competitive advantage. If on the other hand the R&D is borne exclusively, or to a large extent, by business this knowledge can be sold anywhere in the world, and with our ridiculously harsh patent and copyright

laws, this precludes local industries from benefiting from it for many years. This does not serve national interests well.

Some R&D projects are too expensive for business to undertake, so government needs to fund them. This may also involve inter-government cooperation. R&D is critical to the future growth of every economy, so government needs to play a leading role.

Indirect government involvement as described above (in the form of trade protection, support/incentives and R&D) is important for business and the economy. This involvement is only possible if we have big governments, capable of reviewing and assessing the market carefully and applying resources effectively.

Governments must take action now.
Governments must act now in making investments (as suggested in this chapter) which will strengthen their long-term economic prospects and the quality-of-life of their citizens. Government investment in infrastructure, education, technology and R&D underpinned growth. This makes private investment more attractive, as they have a strong active economy.

Naturally, funding will be the first issue. They must not hesitate in raising taxes (provided they have the political will, and foresight to do so.) They must target those who have benefited the most from manipulating our economy. They are the ones with the money, and able to pay. It's now time for them to pay back what they have taken. Those to be taxed include:-
1) The rich, together with clamping down on tax avoidance and evasion,
2) Corporations, particularly those who do not invest, and stockbrokers,
3) Rent seekers, in their many guises, but particularly the financial sector and gambling companies.
4) Those who are causing environmental damage and degradation.
5) Companies who have benefited from free markets, or are using regulations unfairly to protect their interests (i.e. corporate welfare.)

When people see taxes imposed on these people/entities, it restores their faith in a broken system. It encourages everybody to play fair and not to try and cheat the system. Right now, the majority see top earners pay less pro rata tax, which is unfair. Therefore, they have no compunction in trying to cheat the system. Why play by the rules that don't serve you?. This changes all that.

At the same time as increasing taxes, government must make it clear that their intention is to no longer support free markets, but rather to build a strong national economy. This will mean that any corporate relocation elsewhere, to escape tax increases, will not enjoy access to the national economy on the same terms and conditions as those who pay their taxes and invest in the national economy.

It will be a long, hard road to dismantle the systems, procedures and laws put in place to benefit vested interest, but it needs to be done. The sooner, the better. Over time, as new systems, procedures and laws are introduced to help national economies serve the needs of the majority, then harsh taxes on corporates and the wealthy can be removed to reflect these changes.

Austerity - another devious manipulation.
I need to raise the issue of austerity, as it affects most people living in developed economies. It's the main reason for plummeting quality-of-life. Austerity means governments are spending less on providing social support services and investing less in infrastructure. All the things which provide a high quality-of-life. These cutbacks mean governments are becoming much smaller.

That's precisely what the wealthy one per cent want. They want small governments, so to achieve this they have concocted a message to support this objective, which they then promote vigorously. Consequently, it's now a message which resonates around the world. They draw an analogy between government budgets and that of households. If a household overspends, they must cut back on expenditure to balance their budget. The same is true for governments, so they claim. People can understand this and think it's true. However, the analogy is entirely incorrect. Governments are different from individuals as an individual's income is generally fixed. They can do little to change this; they are between "a rock and a hard place", with fixed incomes and rising costs, their only option is to cut costs. However, a government's income is not fixed, and they can do a lot to improve income (or revenue.)

By reducing government expenditure, this impacts negatively on the economy, reducing revenues even further, adding impetus to austerity. Austerity does not bring about recovery, it brings about more austerity. It results in smaller government - meaning the wealthy one per cent have achieved their objective. Smaller governments play a smaller role in the economy and society. They can no longer serve the needs of the majority and are left more vulnerable to further manipulation by the wealthy. Democracy itself starts failing, as we have already seen.

To break austerity, you need to stimulate growth, which the government can do by spending more on society, economy and environment. By spending more on social services, the government invests in so-called "economic stabilisers." This is dealt with in a little more detail in Chapter Seven. Basically, if the government provides it's citizens good social safety nets, and social services, this stabilises the economy as even in the hardest of times, money is recirculated in the economy. Without it, the economy can collapse. Spending money on infrastructure and investing in R & D stimulates growth, pushing up revenues. Investing in protecting the environment also generates revenues and helps protect our future. Such investments will end austerity, but this involves greater government involvement. This means substantially higher taxes on the rich and greater limits on free markets.

Austerity leads to austerity, small governments, the lowering of quality-of-life and the weakening of democracy. An alternative, which sees government investment in social, economic and environmental projects ends austerity, leads to a higher quality-of-life, and strengthens democracy through bigger more involved government. Of course, this needs funding and that's the issue the wealthy one per cent have. They want to retain, and amass their wealth, not spend it on the common good, despite the overwhelming advantages to all of doing so. Their short-term, myopic profit obsession blinds them.

Summary.

The objective of governments is to improve the standard-of-living and quality-of-life of its citizens while protecting the environment. To do this requires the government to deliver many diverse services, all of which cost money. The better they are at meeting their objectives, the bigger their expenditure - the bigger government becomes. So, a big government is a good indicator of its citizen's well-being, whereas a small government is the complete opposite.

Governments which appear to spend less either don't provide the services, in which case their citizens are poorer for this, (bearing the costs of providing the service or foregoing it) or government has shifted their cost onto other parties, in which case the costs are still incurred but hidden.

No matter which way we look at it, meeting government objectives means big expenditure - big government. Governments can try and hide the fact, but to what end? Outsourcing and divesting do not deliver improved quality of service over time; it only denies the government the opportunity to benefit from possible efficiency gains. There are other disadvantages such as strategic threat and weak economic growth.

The claim that big government is bad for the economy is just a ruse by vested interests, to ensure their needs are met, with no regard to others needs and requirements. They don't care about the harm this does, only about their profits and their wealth. Sweden has high tax rates which they use to finance public expenditure, which lead to higher growth than leading developed economies who do not tax or invest in infrastructure.

Those governments who fall for the nonsense that lean governments are more efficient have completely missed the point and guarantee their citizens a lower quality-of-life. They have failed their citizens by following the advice of vested interests. Large governments are not bad for us, to the contrary, they are good. There are dangers that inefficiencies creep into government departments, so a watchful eye needs to be had. All alternatives have their pros and cons, just like big governments. It's just that it's pros considerably outweigh its cons.

Chapter 7
Make small business development a priority.

Business, like you and I go through a life cycle, from birth to death. There are births and deaths every day. Unless there is birth, and unless young people grow up healthy, well adjusted and educated, our society will no longer function properly. The same applies to our economy. We need the birth of new businesses, and they need to grow up healthy, well adjusted and educated, otherwise our economy won't function properly.

To achieve this requires long-term vision and investment by government. However, this is where we encounter a problem because, the masters of our economy, the wealthy one per cent don't operate on the same basis. They see the economy through the prism of short-term outcomes and a narrow vision of investing only in what affects them directly. We, however, understand good outcomes often take time. We also know we live in an interconnected world, where the support and well-being of our fellow citizens and the protection of our environment ultimately benefits all. To prosper, we need to consider all business constituents, not just shareholders. We appreciate it takes time, money and a wider vision to achieve worthwhile outcomes. However, this is in contrast to vested interest's approach of immediate results and only expenditure on matters affecting them directly.

This outlook hinders small business development because it takes long-term vision which involves investment in a broad cross-section of society, which, at first glance may not appear linked to small business development. It involves big government, which vested interests are opposed to. So, they don't have the vision, investment appetite and are vehemently opposed to a fundamental requirement for success - big government. However, there are other reasons they don't want to commit to small business development, despite paying lip service to its need. They don't want to see the entrepreneurial base grow. This means the introduction of new competitors and possibly disruptive practices, which may shake them to their foundations. So, they are keen to hinder the growth of others and the spread of wealth.

Their objective is to ensure wealth remains concentrated in their hands.

However, we aren't interested in vested interests needs and concerns, but those of the majority. To this end, we have to see the importance of small business development in the same light as we see education. Both play a critical role in broadening our economic base and thus our standard-of-living and quality-of-life. From well supported small business giants grow. We must create the fertile ground for future big business to grow. Most of the biggest and most profitable giants of today were until recently small start-ups - garage businesses. Although the majority will never grow to such lofty heights, they should grow and become significant contributors to our economy and society, and that's what we need.

It takes time, money and a broad vision to grow our economy. It's about broadening the base and including more people in the entrepreneurial class. Getting more people to start and run successful businesses. Strong competition and strong innovation – that's what grows the economy not reinvesting in current processes and yesterday's thinking, which is how vested interest wants it to remain.

First building block.

Developing small business does not start with training, funding or support as so many believe. It begins by creating a society which provides social support in the form of decent unemployment benefits, health benefits, housing support, and pension support. This environment makes the prospects of failure less onerous. Nobody starts out to fail, but if we minimise the risks associated with failure, more will undertake the risk. That's the first building block and one vigorously opposed by vested interests. They attack it because it involves a higher tax burden on them. They claim this leads to a welfare state where people become lazy. More importantly, it leads to an environment where people are less afraid of change and risk, and this is important for a vibrant and dynamic economy, not only small business.

Second building block.

The second building block involves providing a supportive business environment, encouraging cooperative effort and providing fair access to markets. This approach allows for effective growth progression from micro to small, and small to medium-sized business. We see the problem this lack of infrastructure and cooperation has on small business growth in developing economies. In these economies, micro businesses show signs of early success, but then the influx of competition destroys them. The reasons for this is, early entrants cannot make the transition to the next level and progress up the ladder, allowing space for new entrants. Markets become overcrowded and unprofitable and collapse. Everybody remains at the bottom, and ultimately only a few make a meagre living. Poor infrastructure and cooperation among businesses are to blame for this lack of upward mobility.

In developed economies, we have considerably better supportive business infrastructures. We have financial systems, legal systems, relatively efficient governments, limited corruption, functioning policing, educated labour, advanced technology, effective transport and communication systems, reliable energy supplies. The list goes on. In developing economies most of these services barely exist, or if they do, don't function well. We stand on the shoulders of others in developed economies and can start and run successful micro-businesses because of this; many of which will grow into big businesses. For example, here in the UK, one could start an artisan bakery on one's own, supplying local businesses and community. It could then be fairly easily scaled-up to serve a wider market competitively. However, a micro-bakery in some parts of Africa will find it considerably more difficult to start and scale-up because of this lack of supportive infrastructure. Further, as there are few job prospects in the area, the likelihood of another micro-bakery starting up are high, making the prospects of expansion for the first bakery impossible. The bakery at best may survive, although it probably won't. Such failure is no reflection on the ability of individuals but of poor supportive infrastructure.

There is another aspect to this supportive infrastructure which helps small business in developed economies, and that is cooperation. Similar businesses band together to cooperate with one another to tackle problems too big for an individual business. Establishing cooperative activities in developing economies is often fraught with difficulties not encountered in developed economies. Cooperatives work well in countries with effective governments and legal systems. In other words, where effective infrastructure exists, cooperative agreements can be formed and enforced. In developing economies, this is considerably more difficult. Although there are better chances to work cooperatively in developed economies, governments should support and encourage the many benefits cooperation presents. In Chapter Six, I mentioned a community coming together to provide local wind turbines. This form of cooperation, serving collective interests is excellent. The downside to cooperatives is they may become too big, and exclude others from entering the market; that's why government intervention (regulation) is required.

We must learn the lessons taught us by developing economies, recognising how crucial supportive infrastructure is. Although our supportive infrastructure is far better than developing economies, it's far from perfect and needs to be developed much further. Take our judicial system as an example. In Chapter Three I explained how it is too complex, cumbersome and slow moving, making it costly. This makes it an institution which serves the needs of the rich, not the poor. Small, emerging businesses need an effective and affordable system to help them grow, not a system used to threaten and bully them. Other rent-seeking activities such as money lending and patents, are roadblocks to effective development. So, while developed economies are better than developing economies, they still have a long way to go. In this regard, there are two critical areas we need to work on. First is to allow small business access to bigger markets. Here governments should play a more active role in legislating for it. This legislation would force businesses to source a percentage of their supplies and services from small businesses (should small local businesses exist, and be able to meet requirements.) As soon as this is done, it would be easier for small business to secure development loans (this being a factor which has inhibited their growth in the past) against secure, possibly large contracts. The next important area to address is providing access to funding on reasonable terms. The use of a better measurement standard which provides greater insight into a business's long-term value creation potential will limit investor risk and provide them confidence that the entrepreneur has a clear understanding of what's required to deliver wealth/value for all. Government regulations in providing the framework for funding small businesses is also required.

Governments need to acknowledge the importance of small business and protect their interests against dominant Big Business (some of whom use small businesses to fund their operations by holding back payment for over 120 days.) If anything, small business should be given preferential treatment, with a requirement for their accounts to be settled within 30 days. As small businesses grow, they help keep Big Business in check, spread wealth, create employment, build strong and broad-based economies. It is the nursery of tomorrows Big Business. From these many seedlings, a forest grows. It is likely that in the future most people will work for themselves, or be employed by SMEs (Small Medium Enterprise.) The day of the big corporation may be over. In which case, are we laying the correct foundation for the future? No, we are not, but we can change all that.

Collective entrepreneurship.
The term "collective entrepreneurship" occasionally crops up and people sometimes confuse it with "cooperative entrepreneurship", but it's not the same thing. Cooperative entrepreneurship is something I have already mentioned. So, what's "collective entrepreneurship"? Most of us understand that small businesses rely on their owner/entrepreneur as the main, if not the only, source of leadership. Collective entrepreneurship suggests that a small business should develop "collective entrepreneurial" capabilities by drawing on the talents and creativity of all its employees synergistically creating continuous and incremental innovations. Of course, this should be the case, but the reality is that in many small businesses they consist of only one person for many years. New staff are often employed to perform mundane everyday tasks to free the owner. These people are often not capable of contributing at the same level as the founder/owner.

Nonetheless, if possible, it is a principle which should be adopted because "two heads are better than one." Entrepreneurship is a lonely and difficult place because owners must wear many hats and juggle many tasks, so calling on others to help contribute is important.

We must celebrate the heroic nature of entrepreneurship. These individuals take high risks and work hard. Without them who will initiate change and drive innovation? Only another entrepreneur. We would be a lot poorer without them. We must not minimise their heroic role. They are a special group of people and society should hold them in the highest regard, much like they hold certain professions. If we do that, we light the fires of free enterprise, from which we all benefit.

Third building block.
The third building block deals with the one which everybody starts addressing first, providing training, funding, support, advice and guidance. All very important, but as we have seen, unless the environment is right, you can't achieve the full potential of small business. Gardeners and farmers will be the first to tell you to prepare the ground before planting and tending your crops. The same applies to small businesses.

The bookshelves are creaking under the weight of all the literature on what needs to be done to develop small business. There are also many good organisations dedicated to this end. While this is all good, they often forget the critical part of preparing the fertile ground, which falls beyond the gambit of all their literature, discussion and effort.

Vested interests are also keen on playing down the importance of the first two building blocks. They don't like start-ups and new market entrants, or market disrupters, as they directly threaten their wealth. Typical of vested interests, they mislead us into believing they care and act in our interests when their intention is only the preservation of their wealth. To this end, they play up their involvement in this narrow aspect (the third building block) of small business development, while being fully aware that there are other, more important aspects of small business success which need to be addressed. If these two aspects (building blocks 1 and 2) are not in place, small business development remains problematic. Because of this, small business failure rates remain high; unacceptably high. I believe, in part, vested interests play a major role in this by limiting access to markets and finance, and discouraging new entrants by promoting high failure rate statistics, while making the superficial pretence of supporting small business. They certainly are not keen on big government and making the investment suggested for our first building block.

In developing economies, we see a high level of entrepreneurial activity, much higher than in developed economies. This is because of a lack of employment. This forces people into seeking economic activities on their own, which may produce some income, no matter how meagre. However, because of a lack of supportive infrastructure, this does not lead to an expanding economy, despite the enormous amount of self-employed. So, getting people to enter the entrepreneurial class is ill-advised if the supporting infrastructure is not in place and everything is done to support them. By believing you are helping small business succeed without laying the foundation, is building on sand.

Fourth building block.
There is a fourth building block, and it has to do with wider social support. This social support differs from that mentioned under building block one, which has to do with providing a financial cushion for those who may lose their employment. This building block (the fourth) has to do with all the facets of delivering a high quality-of-life for citizens. This includes, among other things, looking after those not actively involved in the economy due to age or disability. Plus, the provision of community amenities such as libraries, sports/recreational facilities. When we know our society is highly supportive, that we need not worry about our needs, or those of our family, this is highly conducive in producing a vibrant society and productive economy. The more energy people expend on worries, such as educating their children, ensuring they have a safe environment to grow up in and supporting parents, the less they concentrate on their work - the

less productive they become. Stress and anxiety adversely affects productivity.

Building blocks one and four have an equal impact on all business activity, big and small, and thus positively influence economic growth. Naturally, all these services cost money; they are like any other input cost. It's not the expenditure which should concern us but rather the benefits it delivers. If the benefits outweigh the cost, then the expenditure is justified. This expenditure contributes to growing the economy in the following ways:-

- Directly encourages people's willingness to embrace change. This leads to a dynamic and innovative economy.
- Directly contributes to a contented, willing workforce, not worried by the vagaries of life.
- Money spent on providing this support remains in our active economy, helping it grow.
- It contributes to a growing and more successful entrepreneurial base, which expands the economy. This helps keep Big Business in check and limits the possible growth of monopolies.
- With good social protection systems in place workers income and consumption are sustained, in the face of market downturns - it provides an economic buffer (referred to as "automatic stabilisers.") Without these economic stabilisers, market downturns adversely affects wages, which amplifies the effects of the downturn on the economy. Without these stabilisers, recovery will be long and hard.

So, while the expenditure is justified in economic terms, it is also building a caring and supportive society, adding to the quality-of-life for all citizens. Countries with less inequality, such as those who invest in social support, provide greater equality of opportunity - this bodes well for the future - inequality decreases. The opposite is equally true.

Vested interests would have us believe this creates a fat, lazy social state. If you see life through a limited prism of immediate results and only investment which benefits you directly, then you may believe them. However, if you have a broader, long-term vision, appreciating the interconnectivity of all, and what benefits others ultimately benefits you, you will have difficulty believing them. A broader, interconnected approach produces substantially better long-term results for the economy and society. The reason this is true is simple - society and economy are interrelated. A strong society - a strong economy, and vice versa. Vested interests try to hide this fundamental truth, by calling it socialism. However, the facts are, when you serve the needs of all participants, not just a select participant or group of participants, Capitalism thrives. It recognises a fundamental truth that you require balance - imbalanced systems eventually collapse. Therefore, it favours and supports the fair reward of all. Capitalism recognises the importance of generating profits for shareholders, but it's not its objective. Rewarding every participant fairly is a fundamental principle of Capitalism. Profit represents shareholder reward, and without sustained long-term profits business collapses, but not rewarding other participants fairly will also result in failure. Fair reward for all guarantees the future growth of Capitalism.

We are not socialists because we acknowledge the importance of providing social support for a strong economy. We are realists who want to build a strong, broad, inclusive economy, which serves the many, not just an elite few. We acknowledge this costs money and takes time, but it does work. We recognise the need for big government. We do not spread disinformation and attempt to pervert actions which are in the interests of the majority, in order to horde wealth generated by profiteering from one's own stakeholders.

Summary.
An important way of expanding the economy, spreading wealth, keeping Big Business in check and fanning the fires of free enterprise is to foster and grow small business. The more seedlings we plant, the bigger the forest of new businesses.

This requires a long-term vision and significant investment, particularly in social support. This means big government. This not only benefits small business but all business, leading to a more dynamic and stronger economy, where the standard-of-living and quality-of-life for all improves.

Vested interests vehemently fight against this because it will see their wealth dissipated and spread more evenly. They fight this by spreading misinformation and using their power and influence in every way possible to retain their wealth and influence; to restrict the growth of competition.

Chapter 8
Stop chasing unmanaged growth.

The mantra chanted by most politicians and governments today is that as long as GDP (Gross Domestic Product) growth is good, things are good, because there's increased revenue to meet liabilities. If there's no growth or a decline, that's bad – very bad. This belief is entirely wrong. and therefore, a reckless policy to follow. Chasing GDP without due financial consideration is pure insanity. If the underlying financials do not support growth, then growth hurts the average citizen - it does not benefit them. So growth under all circumstances is crazy nonsense. Only managed growth is beneficial.

There are strong similarities between a business over-trading and governments chasing GDP growth without due consideration for critical, underlying financial considerations, which if ignored, leaves the majority of citizens considerably worse off. Just as it's bad for business to chase sales, ignoring the same financial considerations, so to is it financially reckless for governments to chase GDP growth.

So, if it's "insanity" to chase GDP growth without due consideration of the underlying financials, why do we do it? Because, it's another lie fed us by vested interests to serve their needs not ours. One of the most effective ways of influencing public opinion is to influence and shape politician's thoughts as they are influential in determining policy. They, like the general public, are bombarded by vested interest to modify their perceptions. To see things from their perspective and to influence policy accordingly. It's not about the truth and reality, but about perceptions created to support their one-sided interests. It's in the wealthy one per cent's interest to have the economy keep on growing as it supports their sales and profit. So, naturally they tell us that GDP growth is essential for our economy and our well-being. Like all their other lies, they promote them vigorously, until they enter our conscious mind and we quote them as if they are some law of nature - "we need GDP growth." However, would vested interests invest in any business who is knowingly over-trading? Of course not, because it spells financial disaster and business failure. They won't knowingly over-trade, but they encourage governments to chase GDP growth, in the full knowledge that it will create financial misery if the underlying financials cannot support growth. They do it out of self-interest, with no regard to the hardships the citizens of the country will face as a consequence. We have to get politicians to see the light and stop singing vested interests tune, which inflicts harm on their constituents.

Businesses prove that by cutting back sales, and improving their financial situation is a far more prudent strategy to follow. The same applies to governments. Cutting back on GDP growth can benefit rather than harm, as I will explain. Governments need to grow at a sustainable financial rate, as do businesses, otherwise they over-trade and fail.

When a business over-trades it invariably goes under because their financial growth was not planned correctly and as a result they run out of cash. Governments can get into a similar "over-trading" situation, but rather than go under, they increase their borrowings, thereby increasing their costs, which worsens their financial position. Increased borrowing over an extended period eventually forces the government into an "austerity programme" involving severe cost cutting. Unfortunately, governments don't address the underlying causes, so their austerity programmes have to become even more austere and last longer - indefinitely, until the fundamentals are addressed. Such austerity programmes hurt society and drastically lower the quality-of-life for most citizens.

The UK, is a case in point, it has been "over-trading", and continues to do so, thereby perpetuating their austerity programme; this is because the fundamentals of the problem have been ignored. Citizens quality-of-life has dropped over the decades and will continue to fall. Similar situations exist elsewhere, most notably in Greece. This is a major problem and a screw-up which needs to be fixed as it directly effects the quality-of-life for the majority.

What's over-trading?

So what is over-trading and how does a government over-trade, as it cannot be classified as a trading entity? First, lets understand how business over-trades and then draw similarities with government. Business over-trades when it chases sales but does not have the cash resources, or access to further borrowings, or equity to fund the increased sales. As a result, the business's cash dries up and it is forced out of business.

Increased sales come at a cost. Business has to find additional resources to fund growth. Take the example of an imaginary business shown below, to demonstrate where cash is tied up in a business.

Raw Material stock holding	+ 15 days
Production cycle	+ 5 days
Finished stock holding	+ 25 days
Debtor days	+ 50 days
Creditor days	- 35 days
Conversion Cycle	= 60 days

If the business wishes to increase sales it has to find cash to fund this 60 day cycle, called the "Cash Conversion Cycle". So, on average, this business only gets their cash back in 60 days. They have to find cash to fund new sales for up to 2 months.

Every business has a "Cash Conversion Cycle" (CCC), which is a measure of its short-term cash-flow requirements. There are many things a business can do to reduce its CCC, which means it will require less cash to fund growth and can therefore grow faster. The longer the cycle the more working capital the business requires, the slower its growth.

Funding Working Capital.

Because every new sale has to be funded through increased Working Capital (except for those businesses with a negative CCC. Certain businesses, such as cash retailers, who buy on credit and have a high stock-turn, may experience a negative CCC where increasing sales reduces their Working Capital requirements.) Ideally, growth should be funded out of profits. The extent to which a business can fund its growth through profit is called it's "sustainable growth rate." If it exceeds this, cash-flow starts drying up. Cash dries up in proportion to the extent that sustainable growth is exceeded. If a business exceeds this rate, then it has to borrow or raise equity to fund the increase in working capital to prevent a cash flow crisis.

Sales expansion often goes hand-in-hand with increased infrastructure expansion, such as increased expenditure on R & D, production facilities (machinery/buildings,) storage, distribution, sales, marketing and promotions. These involve additional expenditure, which add to costs and reduce profitability, thereby reducing its sustainable growth rate and the business's ability to fund working capital.

Where a business's margins are low and they require infrastructure expansion to meet additional sales, they are particularly vulnerable to market downturns. In downturns margins come under competitive attack and are often reduced. Costs could also rise unexpectedly. Under such circumstances, their margins may be inadequate to produce a profit to service their increased infrastructure costs. They will obviously cutback costs where they can but some infrastructure costs may be medium or long-term, meaning they can't reduce costs enough. If the downturn lasts, they will face a cash flow crisis and will, in all likelihood, fail.

Key issues in preventing over-trading.
For a business to ensure it does not over-trade it needs to:-
- Optimise it's CCC (i.e. reduce its working capital through greater efficiencies,) and
- Improve margins and therefore, profits (although this is not easy.)
- Not exceed their sustainable growth rate, and
- Ensure infrastructure expansion can be supported through a serious and sustained downturn, preferably funded through retained income, borrowings or increased equity. However, it's unlikely any business will be able to borrow or raise equity if they have ignored the three preceding financial considerations.

Businesses who chase sales, irrespective of these key issues, will fall victim to over-trading and fail.

Governments who chase GDP growth without due consideration for the same key issues will have to borrow to survive, thereby worsening their financial position and will eventually introduce austerity programmes to cut costs. Most will not address the underlying financial causes, so austerity deepens and continues until the fundamentals are addressed. Downgrading or cutting services, the result of austerity programmes, lowers the quality-of-life for the average citizen. Every year these austerity programmes continue, there is a progressive decline in quality-of-life. The responsibility of government is to build quality-of-life, not destroy it by chasing GDP growth.

Government equivalents.
Governments don't use the same language to refer to the same things in business, so let's look at the government equivalents for these key financial considerations, which if not managed effectively will ultimately lead to cuts and extended austerity programmes.

CCC equates to Departmental efficiencies.
Businesses must use their working capital more efficiently (i.e. optimise their CCC) to improve profit, and therefore, their ability to fund growth. Governments are no different. They to must manage their departmental resources more efficiently, which leads to an improved surplus, or helps reduce their deficit. Just as a business's profit dictates it growth, so to does a governments surplus dictate government growth. If a government grows off a deficit their borrowings increase, so to their costs, with a reduction in their sustainable growth rate. Continued expansion off a deficit, compounds the problem. Therefore, it starts by ensuring government uses their resources efficiently, otherwise, they will deplete their surplus (should they have one) and increase their borrowings.

Profit margin equates to tax margins.
If business makes too little profit from a sale, because of small margins, its sustainable growth rate will be low. It can only grow slowly. Furthermore, if growth requires infrastructure expansion, involving medium to long-term debt, the business is at high risk of failing.

Governments are in the same position. If they have a low tax margin, i.e. where their revenue barely covers their cost, they can only expand slowly. If they expand beyond the rate of their surplus, their borrowings will increase and so to their costs. At this point, their costs may exceed revenue, putting them into a deficit. Future growth can now only be funded through borrowings, as there is no surplus. The situation gets progressively worse, year-on-year because of their reliance on borrowing to fund growth. Their debt just keeps mounting. Continuous expansion requires increased infrastructure support. This places the finances under even more pressure, increasing government debt even more. To stop the hole getting even bigger, governments go on drastic cost cutting programmes. This negatively impacts on the average citizens quality-of-life. Business, under these circumstances would immediately cut back sales (growth), cut costs where they can and not undertake any infrastructure programmes, as well as limited maintenance of infrastructure. They would then consider ways of improving their margins. Governments on the other hand trundle along making very few critical adjustments, apart from cutting costs. The key thing to do is increase taxes (margin.)

Address poor tax margins.
The increasing divide between rich and poor is an indication of government's inadequate tax policy, particularly concerning corporate and personal tax of the rich. During the Reagan presidency in America (1981 - 1989) he was responsible for supporting and introducing neoliberal economic policies, such as privatisation, deregulation, free trade and reducing the size of government. Reagan lowered taxes on the wealthy from 70% to only 28% and broke the air traffic union strikes, which saw the weakening of collective bargaining. He had a major influence on Margaret Thatcher (UK Prime Minister from 1979 to 1990) who

followed his neoliberal economic policies. She reduced the tax rate from 83% on the wealthy to 60% which has subsequently been lowered to 45%. She also broke the strength of the trade unions. This is the era when the rot set in. These legacies live on in today's politicians as they follow neoliberal economic policies based on the misinformation fed them of how it serves our needs when the proof that it does not is evident all around us. The point I want to make here is that we do not tax the wealthy adequately. Top tax rate should return to the pre-Reagan era and be set at over 70% as suggested by leading economist Emmanuel Saez, Thomas Piketty and Stefanie Stantchev. This would go a long way in lifting tax margins. However, corporate welfare and the welfare of the rich is deeply embedded in our tax codes. Because of this, and a low top tax rate, we have a regressive tax system where the rich pay less tax pro rata than the average person. What we have is a tax system which starts too low (the tax threshold should be much higher, meaning the poor won't pay any tax.) It then rises too quickly and flattens out too quickly, ending up at a top rate far too low. Such a tax structure places the burden on the masses. What it should do is start high, increase gradually and then begin increasing rapidly, ending in a high top rate. This would ensure top earners carry the biggest tax burden, which is how a balanced economy should work. We have the wealth and resources to eliminate poverty and improve everybody's quality-of-life, but can do little about it when resources are held by one per cent of the population, who do not contribute their fair share.

As we have seen throughout this book, businesses are given almost unfettered access to national and global resources to enrich shareholders. They develop systems and procedures to ensure their interests are protected, which includes using their power to influence policy makers in minimising their taxes, at our expense. We are fed rubbish like, "if we over-tax corporates or the rich, they will go elsewhere to do business." This might sound plausible, but the reality is business is attracted to where the market is, and if we have a strong economy then businesses are attracted to that. By not taxing corporates and the rich adequately, this redirects resources out of the active economy into the rentier economy, weakening the active economy thereby shrinking the economy and making it less attractive. These actions adversely affect the average citizens quality-of-life. So, by taxing corporates and the rich more appropriately, will address the tax margin problem and the inequality of our economic systems, as well as improve our active economy. Some may believe this will be political suicide to increase taxes, but to the contrary, they are facing political suicide by not addressing the problem of low tax margins. How long do people, who are adversely affected by austerity programmes, which make up the majority, go on accepting these cuts, until they call for radical change?

The Brexit scenario.

Brexit presents an interesting and unique scenario in considering what growth policy a government should follow. Brexit means change. Change means uncertainty. Uncertainty reduces growth prospects. A "soft" Brexit means less uncertainty whereas a "hard" Brexit more uncertainty, and therefore, lower growth prospects.

Those who believe that "growth is essential" (irrespective of the underlying financials) would favour a soft Brexit. However, given the state of the British economy, is growth advisable or is consolidation the more prudent option?

If viewed purely from a financial perspective, growth would mean "over-trading" and therefore ill-advised. This is based on the following facts. The British economy:-

- Runs on a deficit
- This is indicative of poor tax margins.
- Growth will be funded out of borrowings.
- This will add to the national debt and increase costs, placing greater pressure on the need for cost savings.
- However, the government has had a long-running austerity programme, so the probability of wringing out more savings, or greater efficiencies, is remote. Further savings will therefore only be found through service cuts. This will result in the lowering of citizens quality-of-life. In fact, the only costs which can be cut out which won't affect quality-of-life are inefficiencies. Other cost reductions will result in the lowering of service standards, which equates to a lowering of quality-of-life.

These are the harsh realities British citizens face in chasing growth.

If on the other hand a hard Brexit were implemented and again, viewed purely from a financial perspective, it would favour British citizens. I will discuss the difficulties of adopting a strictly financial perspective afterwards, but first, let's look at the reasons why it will benefit British citizens.

A hard Brexit, which does not extend residency rights to EU citizens provides the government with a unique opportunity to reduce its net population substantially (whether this is politically or morally desirable is another issue.) This would enable the government to lower its cost base significantly. It also means its revenues will be reduced significantly. However, because British tax margins are marginal (producing no surplus), the lost revenue will have no impact on the fiscal account. It will, however, mean that infrastructure will be under less pressure, with no need to expand it. This means no additional borrowings will be incurred, with a possible reduction in costs. This would leave the economy in a better financial position, which any hard-nosed businessperson would approve of. However, a fundamental, and critical issue remains – tax margins are too low and need addressing to produce a surplus.

Purely from a financial perspective, a hard Brexit is more favourable to British citizens as it will not result in the lowering of their quality-of-life, in fact, it will improve it (for reasons mentioned above and because infrastructure will be under less pressure.) However, as I said earlier, decisions cannot be based purely on financials (although important.) A hard Brexit would probably result in a significant drop in GDP. The financial world won't view this favourably, and it would adversely affect the value of the Pound, despite the economy being in a better state. This will result in rising costs (of imports) driving up inflation, which is not good for British citizens.

Catch 22 problem and GDP.

This is a Catch 22 problem where the government can't do what's right for their economy and citizens because it's part of a bigger global system and problem. Vested interest does not restrict their meddling to national economies; it's global. They have got us to accept the importance of their measures, which dictate the outcomes they want globally. GDP is the macroeconomic measure we are evaluated against. A measure which favours them. They want national economies to grow in terms of goods and services, irrespective of the damage it causes their economies because over the short-term it means greater profits for them. If we don't grow our GDP, we are punished, yet it's a stupid measure on which to evaluate an economy. It's like evaluating a business on its sales alone. If you do that, prepare yourself for some nasty, and costly surprises. However, the secret to controlling outcomes is to create measures which give you the results you want. We see this at a microeconomic level through our business measurement standard and at a macroeconomic level through GDP measures. Both are inadequate and inappropriate, but they serve the needs of vested interests, so that's why we keep them. In 1990 they changed the measurement standard from GNP (Gross National Product) representing the gross income of the citizens of a country to that of GDP (Gross National Product.) GDP represents the value of goods and services produced within a country. The switch occurred at a time when the pace of globalisation was increasing. This was to show the benefits of globalisation in a good light, which GNP would not have. By using GDP, we are doing as much harm to our society and economy as using an inadequate and inappropriate business measurement standard. It measures what's important for the one per cent and ignores important social and environmental aspects. What you don't measure you don't manage. It's a terrible standard and needs changing.

I've used the Brexit scenario to indicate how a significant drop in GDP could be beneficial to the economy by placing it on a better financial footing. To show how this counts for nothing, and how the British economy would be "punished" as a consequence. I'm not making any political suggestions as to what option to follow. I'm using it because of its unique circumstances in demonstrating how a major drop in GDP would be better than growth and how irrespective of citizens needs, we are forced to grow or be punished. We are punished by an inadequate and inappropriate measure - GDP. A measure which only serves the needs of the wealthy one per cent. This is an appalling state of affairs.

It's also difficult to address the crucial issue of inadequate tax margins in a so-called "free global market" where funds and businesses can relocate with relative ease. Until we limit this free movement by making access to vacated markets more difficult, then vested interests have us over a barrel. When we restrict market access, we make relocation decisions a lot harder. We take away their negotiating strength over national economies. Governments can then raise taxes on corporates and the wealthy with only minor repercussions. Over the past four decades, by strengthening their negotiating position, vested interests have manoeuvred their way into a position where they are able to have their taxes reduced . It's now time to declare - "game over."

The one per cent - winners under all circumstances.
Most people believe that growth and austerity are directly linked. Austerity is a consequence of a lack of growth. This is untrue - a lie, fostered by the one per cent. Austerity is a (misused) policy, it's not a consequence of a lack of growth. Growth and austerity are unrelated. Austerity is a policy or mechanism, whose prime objective is to reduce the size of government. This is a crucial objective of the one per cent (as explained in Chapter Six - "Austerity - another devious manipulation.") The reality is, austerity only worsens austerity, it does not result in growth. Austerity is cured through economic stimulus, which the government can provide through spending on things like social security, infrastructure and R&D. The complete opposite of what the one per cent want.

Now, look at how cleverly and deviously they have manipulated government and perceptions to serve their needs under all circumstances. They force governments to grow as that benefits them. They are the primary cause for the government having poor underlying financials, which means growth worsens the government's financial position and drives austerity harder. The one per cent benefit through austerity. They benefit through growth and austerity. The majority - the ninety-nine per cent, lose on both accounts. Even if there is no growth, the one per cent "win" as austerity remains, which benefits them. The majority still lose on both accounts - there are no growth benefits, and austerity continues. This is a sad state of affairs, which is easily rectified.

Growth is not the issue - quality-of-life is.
Since 2000 in the UK we've had GDP growth (with a few exceptions) but quality-of-life over this period has not improved, but declined? How can this be, if growth is supposed to benefit us? The majority are suffering under persistent austerity with no prospect of improvement. The facts are, growth does not benefit us, particularly if it occurs off weak financials. Vested interests are the main reason government financials remain weak, and they are also the ones forcing us to grow. As we are now, GDP growth will keep hurting the majority, while only serving the needs of vested interest. We don't have to grow our economy, it can even shrink (under certain circumstances,) and we will be better off. What our economy is supposed to do is serve the majority by improving their quality-of-life, not destroying it. This is its objective, which it should achieve whether the economy grows or not.

Summary.
A belief that GDP growth is good under all circumstances is a reckless and dangerous policy to follow. Growth is only good if it can be funded correctly – if not, then growth can do more harm than good. It has the potential of destroying economies and with it the quality-of-life for most citizens.

However, it is vested interests who promote the idea that continuous growth is good, no matter what, as it serves their agenda. This, even though they would never advocate the same approach for their investments. They realise it's a foolhardy strategy to chase growth without due consideration of the underlying financial position of their investment.

Governments who chase GDP growth are now paying the price through long-running austerity programmes and high borrowings. They have to get their fundamentals in place or quality-of-life will keep sliding. First, ditch the idea that GDP growth is of paramount importance. It's not a good indicator of anything meaningful, like quality-of-life, which should be one of governments key objectives. Manage growth carefully and do not be afraid of not growing, if it cannot be funded prudently. I know this will be frowned upon, but when will the madness of unmanaged growth be addressed?

Governments are cutting costs and trying to improve efficiencies, but the big step they need to address is the improvement of their tax margins. They must increase corporate taxes and taxes on the wealthy. This will be difficult as this is a very influential group, and will do everything to fight it. However, there must be the political will to do so, in conjunction with other changes which will limit vested interest from holding governments to ransom over taxes, which they have been able to reduce over the decades. The widening rich/poor divide is proof that they are under contributing and that it's time for change.

Chapter 9
Encourage manufacturing.

There is a belief, mainly fostered by vested-interest, that developed economies progress from a predominantly manufacturing-base to a service-based economy. While there is a shred of truth to this, to believe that the loss of one's industrial-base is a natural progression, is entirely wrong, misleading and damaging to national economies. Vested interests benefit directly by promoting this idea. They benefit by promoting free markets, which enables them to produce anywhere in the world where production costs are low, and then sell it back to us at maximum profit. Globalisation is beneficial to vested interests, not national economies or their citizens. Losing ones manufacturing base has many disadvantages, and represents a major screw-up. Vested interests want you to believe there is nothing to worry about the loss of ones manufacturing base as service industries replace them. This is just a ruse to hide the damaging effects of losing ones manufacturing base, which are not replaced by service industries. This is another example of misleading information fed us to further their aims with no regard to the damaging consequences felt by national economies both socially and economically. Like most of their other misleading lies, they promote it extensively until many believe the message to be true. Politicians and other influencers take up the cudgels and fight vested interests cause, ignorant of the damage they are doing to their constituents and economy.

The facts are, we consume, in great measure and will continue to do so. We buy food, clothes, cars, TVs, gadgets, appliances - the list goes on, and on. These products have to be produced somewhere. Much is not produced nationally, but internationally. When we import more than we export we incur a deficit in our balance of payments. More money leaves the country than enters. This has to be financed. A sustained deficit leads to increased borrowings, which leads to increased costs, which leads to a lowering of the quality-of-life, as governments implement spending cuts to reduce expenditure.

As the industrial base grows so too does the service sector. Unfortunately, the opposite does not hold true - when the service sector grows, manufacturing does not necessarily grow. This is because services do not induce economic activity to the same degree manufacturing does. Manufacturing offers growth opportunities to service providers through the manufacturing process and their worker needs. It also creates export opportunities by allowing the service sector to acquire knowledge and expertise developed around an industry or industries. This knowledge and expertise can then be exported to other countries in need of it. However, it must be appreciated that it's far more difficult to export services than manufactured goods. Service exports are limited to highly specialised knowledge and skills, often related to manufacturing. Therefore, a shrinking manufacturing base limits the ability to acquire such knowledge and expertise, resulting in a drop in service exports. It also follows, if the service sector grows from a growing manufacturing base, it will shrink when the manufacturing shrinks.

Can services really replace manufacturing?
The big question is, "Can the service sector create enough jobs to replace those lost in the manufacturing sector, and earn enough foreign currency to stop incurring a trade deficits?" Vested interests tell us we can, and not to worry. However, the correct answer is no - never and we should be very concerned at the loss of manufacturing. To start with, the absolute values of goods and services exported are vastly different. For example, in the UK, where the service sector is strong, the value of service exports is only about a third of the value of manufactured goods. Therefore, the service sector has to grow significantly to offset any contraction in manufacturing. Furthermore, the UK's service surplus is limited to financial, engineering and computing services, where current competition is limited, coming only from the US, Germany and Japan. It's foolish to believe these surpluses will keep making up for deficits in manufacturing. Competition will increase, not only from current competitors but from emerging economies like India as a potential software giant. What's more, a shrinking manufacturing base limits the development of multi-disciplinary expertise associated with an industry, reducing service exports further. Brexit may also

adversely affect the UK's financial services. Advances in AI (Artificial Intelligence) may negatively impact service exports. Highly technical jobs with numerous inputs and possible outputs, which previously required highly qualified individuals, are ideally suited to AI, as computers can "crunch" far more possibilities, with a higher degree of accuracy. They are also capable of making "intelligent" decisions based on these possibilities. Computers will give us productivity gains humans cannot, thereby reducing service export potential.

There are many disadvantages associated with services, particularly its low tradability and limited productivity growth. Most services are non-tradable so a strong service sector in comparison with manufacturing will mean poor exports and a balance of payment deficit. A balance of payment deficit limits the country's ability to import technologies which will enable it to compete more effectively, which in turn leads to slower growth. Manufacturing lends itself to mechanisation and therefore productivity gains, whereas it's difficult to improve service productivity without loss of quality. For example, a waiter may serve five tables well but ten poorly. Productivity is gained at the loss of quality. The same applies to services which are exportable. Markets require productivity gains with no loss in quality. This is difficult to achieve for services. Consequently, when an economy becomes dominated by the service sector, productivity growth will be low - the whole economy slows down.

Because service exports are limited to specialised fields with limited productivity growth and earned in an uncompetitive market (which will soon become increasingly more competitive,) and with rapidly developing AI technologies, service exports will shrink, not grow. The only question we need to answer is, "by how much?"

Importance of manufacturing.
We are consumers and will remain so. This requires manufacturing. So manufacturing will always play a major role in our economic life. We will either have to make it or import it. The more we produce, the more money remains in the national economy. The more direct and indirect jobs we create. Local

service providers spring up around manufacturing facilities. These local service providers, although essential to the economy have no impact on exports. Services, generally, evolve around manufacturing, so services cannot "overtake" the importance of manufacturing. Services will grow and become more significant, but never in a leading role - that role belongs to manufacturing. This I believe, is the fundamental relationship between manufacturing and services. Manufacturing provides the leading edge in every economy, and always will. Manufacturing induces economic activity across a broad front. Services don't. Therefore, to lose ones manufacturing base is a grave mistake. The economy which retains the largest manufacturing base will have the strongest economy, and vice versa.

So, to claim its good for us, and a natural progression (in developed economies) to move from a manufacturing base to a service-base is wrong. Its the language used to promote free markets and globalisation. It's supposedly "sophisticated and modern" to think in these terms, but it's extremely misleading and harmful. They paint the picture that manufacturing is a low-level endeavour (dirty, mucky, unsophisticated) better suited to developing countries, not modern, sophisticated countries. Nothing could be further from the truth.

Globalisation and liberalism.
We need to be clear on two concepts which vested interests promote as they are central to their strategy for optimising their wealth, but harmful to the rest of us. They revolve around the concepts of globalisation and liberalism. These are catchy phrases which strike a chord with modern society. We want to think of ourselves as global - interconnected and open-minded - liberal thinkers. We warm to terms like globalisation - it sounds good. Interconnected global trade and cooperation, compared to national self-interest, which sounds backward and inward-looking, nothing to do with modern forward thinking. The same applies to liberalism. We would rather be called liberal than narrow-minded, as liberalism implies mental agility, an ability to appreciate multiple ideas. To accept different ideas.

Free market economics has another name it's called "neo-liberalism" - new liberalism. What they want is for the government to liberate business, take away restrictive laws and allow business to operate freely from government intervention. In reality, what they want is for governments to take away restrictive laws, allowing them to produce and trade anywhere in the world, but retain all the other restrictive laws which protect their wealth. In fact, with increased power and influence they demand greater protection for their wealth, and lower taxes. This is not liberal thinking but devious manipulation. It represents economic enslavement, or economic apartheid - you choose which term you think is appropriate.

This neo-liberalism is the foundation of globalisation. Globalisation has none of the glamour or glitz one may associate with an interconnected, and cooperative world. It results in winners and losers for national economies. The only real long-term winners are the wealthy one per cent, who use global resources to produce low and sell high, thus optimising their profits, while dodging national taxes, by locating head offices in tax havens. Nothing glamorous about that. How many people in developed economies are suffering from austerity, while the rich grow richer in leaps and bounds.

We need to be clear on the importance and value of nationalism and weary of liberalism for reasons I explain below.

National interests.
I want to draw an analogy between a family and government because, we often expect the government to act differently to how we behave towards our family, and yet, the responsibilities are similar. A family, like the government, has limited funds. Your priority as the family head is to ensure you look after family members with these limited funds. Should your funds extend beyond family needs, then you may help wider family and friends. The greater your funds, the further you may spread your generosity. As the family head, it would be unlikely that you would take in people off the street and look after them if such an act would adversely affect your ability to meet family needs - their

food, housing, clothing, health, education, entertainment needs, etc.

However, some people support borderless societies and call for governments to open their borders and take in new immigrants. However, that's not what they do in their own life. They place the interests of their own family first, and rightly so. Why then call on the government to act differently? A government has the same responsibilities to look after its citizens first. If by taking in new immigrants its funds are stretched, this adversely affects the quality-of-life for its citizens. Family and national interests must always come first. This is a basic human instinct, to protect one's own. It's an instinct we should project through our governments. "Putting America first", or "Making America great" are not slogans Americans should cringe from, which many do. They think it's a backward, inward-looking approach - what nonsense. Nationalism is not just about restricting immigration, but also about nurturing and protecting national business interests, particularly manufacturing.

Liberalism.

Despite the innate instinct to protect one's own, "liberal" ideas abound. It's possible to be liberal minded when one is isolated from the effects of one's liberal ideas. For example, supporting a borderless society when one is isolated from its negative effects. If the influx of migrants over-stretches infrastructure, causing withdrawal, reduction or failure of services, and one has the financial resources to protect oneself from these consequences, then one can afford to be liberal minded. If on the other hand, they affect one directly or one's family, and harshly, then one won't be liberal-minded about the effects.

Therefore, liberal ideas must be tempered not by the impact such decision have on one personally, but its impact on the average citizen - national interest. It's often difficult to stand in other's shoes, particularly if you are not well acquainted with their life, or lifestyle. For an affluent person to imagine the lifestyle of the average person, and what the impacts their liberal ideas may have on them would be difficult to appreciate. For liberal-minded individuals, a "unified Europe" where we are all "true Europeans" may appear to be something to work towards. However, there is a massive disparity between nations wealth and the quality-of-life within Europe. To be a unified, equal Europe requires that all share the same quality-of-life. The burden in achieving this upliftment will be carried by the affluent nations for decades to come until some parity exists. However, it won't be the rich from the affluent society who feel the pinch, in fact, they may benefit, but rather the average person. It won't be so much that the average citizen from poorer nations will see massive improvements in their quality-of-life, but a lowering of affluent societies average citizens quality-of-life, to meet in the middle. Only the rich, shielded from these changes will enjoy the benefits. Why should affluent nations citizens (who are not affluent) bear this burden? Are you prepared to drop your family's standards while you help your neighbours improve theirs? So, why expect it of governments? Brexit was a cry from the average person to protect their interests.

Popularism.
Given the effects which free markets and globalisation have on national interests globally, together with liberal ideas, which pay scant regard to national interests, so-called "popularism" is on the rise. Popularism is the manifestation of populace discontent with government direction - ignoring national interests, and stripping nations of their wealth-creation potential. This has led to the lowering of quality-of-life for the majority in developed economies.

We see a populace backlash through Brexit and the election of President Trump, together with the rise of populist parties in Italy. Economists and political observers make comments like "Italy is a wake-up call that populism is alive and well. There was a big wave of optimism after the French election, but the truth is that the problem definitely hasn't gone away." Similar language to this is used glibly by people of the same ilk, referring to nationalism and protectionism as "the problem." However, had they applied only the smallest shred of logic to their thought process, they should have seen that free markets and globalisation is the cause of our problems, because, that's the strategy we've been following for the past four decades. Why on earth would we want to return to what is creating our problems? The populace is right in calling for a change to a system that does not serve their needs. Nationalism and protectionism provide the means by which the average citizen can protect their quality-of-life from the avarice of Big Business and vested interests. Through the strategies of free markets and globalisation, we have seen wages stagnate and manufacturing infrastructure stripped from developed economies. It can't be a return to a strategy that's hurting the average citizen, as misinformed and misguided political leaders (and political commentators) are calling for.

Protectionism.

Big Business and vested interests want you to believe that protectionism is bad because, in the long-term, they claim it weakens the industry through a lack of competition, which means there is no need to innovate. As a consequence, quality drops and prices rise. This is not entirely true, which I will explain shortly. However, without some form of protectionism what happens is industries are lost forever to low-cost production countries. What in your opinion is better for a country - no industry or a poorly performing industry? A poorly performing industry can pull itself together, but a lost industry is just that. You lose the jobs, skills, knowledge and all the services associated with. It's not that easy to bring back a lost industry as it is to improve a struggling one. Often industries are lost because they are not price competitive because of temporary imbalanced labour markets, offered by certain countries. These countries pay wages below the living standard of developed countries, together with poor working conditions. However, over time these will normalise, and prices will go up, but by then we will have lost much of our manufacturing base. This represents a form of global protectionism (or monopoly), where only a few countries will produce the world's manufactured goods. If we are to accept what vested interests say about lack of competition, then this global monopoly, which this is leading towards, will result in quality dropping and prices rising globally. Something we will be unable to influence.

We have to resist succumbing to unfair price advantages as we will pay a dear long-term price. We lose industries not because we cannot compete fairly but because labour conditions around the world vary so much, which vested interests exploit for personal gain, at the cost of national well-being. However, as we mechanise more and more and the labour market normalises (equal pay and working conditions globally) the reasons to produce in faraway places diminishes. Into this equation, you must factor in poorly costed environmental costs of moving goods halfway around the world. In the future, the true environmental costs of moving goods will be taken into account. Using current transport methods would make moving goods produced in faraway places prohibitively expensive. Right now, vested interests don't care about their environmental impact, as long as they are making profits. Unless the environmental impact of transportation is radically reduced, globalisation is non-viable.

Industries become uncompetitive mainly because of imbalanced labour costs, which Big Business and vested interests exploit to optimise profits. This robs local industries of profits and the ability to invest in R&D to develop production methods which would offset "cheap" labour costs. It is here where government need to become involved by providing R&D support and limited protection (in its various forms) to industries under attack from these imbalanced market conditions. Protectionism like this has been used successfully by many countries over many years. Protectionism is like medication. You take it when you are suffering, but stop when you are well, otherwise you become dependent on it and end up weaker as a result. Therefore, to say protectionism is bad is like saying medication is bad. We need it, but need to apply it prudently as a medical doctor prescribes medicine. So rather than being the bogeyman, as vested interests would have it portrayed, protectionism is a critically important tool for governments to protect and resurrect struggling industries or establish new industries. It helps maintain a thriving manufacturing base.

We need to trade with other countries so cannot put up barriers to imports yet expect fair reciprocal exports. Protectionism does present problems and needs to be juggled carefully, but the alternative of free markets and globalisation which destroys the manufacturing base of developed economies is unacceptable. The WTO (World Trade Organisation) is nothing more than a tool used by vested interests to facilitate globalisation. It doesn't address core imbalances in trading conditions, as it's way beyond its scope, yet it is this disparity which vested interests exploit for personal gain at the expense of national economies and their citizens. Developed countries need to take their medication to protect their industries. Obviously, this affects the low labour cost countries, making it more difficult for them to lift their citizens quality-of-life. However, as explained earlier, a government's first responsibility is to protect its own citizens, not those of other countries, just as you look after your family before anybody else. This is not unreasonable - it's human nature.

The flip side of globalisation.
From the viewpoint of a developed economy, globalisation and free markets are bad news. However, for emerging economies, they welcome it as they don't have a strong middle class, and are only concerned with growth, as growth lifts them from poverty and leads to the building of a strong middle class. They grow at the expense of developed economies, because of their low labour costs. They are the winners, and we are the losers.

Globalisation is definitely lifting people out of poverty in emerging economies, and the losers are the middle class in developed economies. These people cannot be classified as rich by a long stretch of the imagination. They don't live in poverty, but neither are they well off. Their quality-of-life is in rapid decline. Why should they bear the burden of uplifting global societies? Their wealthy compatriots pay no price, they only reap the rewards, they do not share this role. A government's first priority is to its citizens. They are failing in their duty by allowing their citizen's quality-of-life to fall. A government is not responsible for the global society. They can and should help, but only from a position of strength. We must not expect a government to do what we as citizens are not prepared to do. Governments are definitely failing their citizens through a complacent/complicit approach to globalisation. Either stop it or make the rich who benefit from it pay for it, not the average citizen. The solution is to stop free markets and globalisation, but this will take time. Therefore, imports need to be taxed harder, and governments need to start investing in local manufacture and R&D as a first step.

We must remember, the things which are wrong can, too a large extent, be changed by the government. We have the power to make them change, as we are the ninety-nine per cent, provided we act collectively. By working collectively, in calling for change as outlined in this book, will be our first step towards a new economy, which acts in the majority's interest. Ensuring government serves all citizens, providing justice for all, fair play and opportunity does not happen by itself. It's continually being moulded. We must ensure we mould it to our requirements.

Summary.
Free markets, globalisation and liberalism, are the scourge of national interests and the average citizen, adversely affecting their quality-of-life. The government's priority is to its citizens not those of other countries. Therefore it has to employ all the tools and strategies available to protect and grow the quality-of-life for the majority of its citizens.

A critically important strategy to follow is to protect and build its manufacturing base because manufacturing forms the foundation of a strong economy, not services. Without a strong manufacturing base the economy will suffer, and with it, the quality-of-life of its citizens will decline, as we have witnessed over the past decades.

Nationalism, protectionism and popularism are not the backward-looking isolationistic mentality, which Big Business and vested interests would like you to believe they are. If you believe them, then you have given them a blank cheque to profit at national expense.

Think about it - only when you are successful can you help others. The more successful you are, the more you can help others. Charity starts at home by making sure you are strong and successful. The same applies to governments. It isn't about withdrawing from the international community to protect your interests but a natural and necessary step to make the nation strong and prosperous so that it can play a meaningful and useful role internationally. If one slides to a point one relies on others for assistance, you are not a contributor, but a burden. The same applies to a nation. To contribute meaningfully means you must be strong and prosperous yourself – national economies must be strong. Do you really believe a massive transnational corporation cares about you and your welfare? They don't give a ##**.

Chapter 10
Realign our higher education system.

There is a misalignment, in developed economies, between the knowledge and skills business require and those produced by our educational institutions. Why should this concern you or I? Because, you may be paying for your, or your child's education, which may not be relevant, or useful. However, there is a wider, more indirect consequence which affects all – an underperforming economy. This leads to a lower quality-of-life for the majority. The blame for this misalignment can be laid directly at vested interests feet. You may think it would be in their interest to ensure education aligns with their (business) needs. This is true, it should, but once again, they put short-term profit ahead of long-term gains. Businesses are evaluated against their short-term financial results. The more they invest in staff training/education the weaker their financials appear over the short-term. Therefore, to serve shareholder and creditor needs, they don't invest, despite knowing of the benefits fully trained and motivated staff produce over the long-term. This explains why business has not taken responsibility for this important facet of business. It's unacceptable because it's hindering economic growth. Rather than invest in staff, they take the money in profits. It may suit their profit needs, but not ours. They are hindering everybody else's well-being for profit.

Fortunately, privately owned and funded businesses are not driven by financial results to the same extent publicly owned and funded businesses are. However, the "disease" of non-investment spreads quickly to them. This is due to the general feeling among businesses that if you invest too heavily in education, you may be making this investment for your competitor's benefit, should staff switch allegiance. Staff are an asset, which you don't own. So, it's a problem if all aren't investing to the same extent, and will remain so while profit is business's sole objective.

Despite the misalignment being foremost a business problem, which they have failed to accept responsibility for, and manage properly, it has led to other parties involved not performing properly. For example, educational institutions believe their institutions are highly effective in preparing students for the workplace, yet only a tiny percentage of businesses (approximately 11%) agree. Research confirms business's misgivings as only a small percentage (35%) feel they are well prepared for the workplace. Further, a significant number of recently qualified graduates (over half) remain unemployed or underemployed. Over 80% of the general public share students view that a four-year degree does not prepare students for a well-paid job. Additional studies show that a significant percentage (40%) of bachelor degree holders would study a different major if they could do it again.

The backdrop to this sorry state is student debt and an ill-prepared workforce. Without a suitably qualified workforce, business is unable to grow and compete. Government is unable to fund a decent quality-of-life for its citizens. Ideally, we should have a highly skilled workforce which is debt free. Instead, we have the complete opposite - this is a major screw-up!

What's causing the problem?

Before I explain a workable solution, let's consider what's causing the problem in a little more detail. There are four key players - business, educational institutions, government and the employee. Business is the primary cause of the problem and unwilling to address it. The problem stems from business's profiteering mindset. As explained in Chapter One, business's objective is to serve shareholder profit interests at the expense of other stakeholders, which includes staff, their education and training needs. Business wants, and expects, fully qualified and capable individuals to be ready to start work immediately without delay. They don't want to outlay any money (or as little as possible) on education or training and want as little or no downtime as possible, as this will adversely affect their profits. New employees must be up and running and productive as soon as possible. Business wants their cake and to eat it. The reality is they can't. Our education and training misalignment is a direct consequence of business's vast underinvestment in its staff. The fact that they have not taken responsibility for, or managed this vital facet of business. Instead, they have relinquished control over it, to optimise profits, for shareholder's benefit. They have shifted responsibility and costs elsewhere, yet complain the process does not work.

Some businesses will argue that if they invest in staff development staff may be poached and their "investment" misplaced as competition will benefit from their "investment". This is a possibility, but that is why we need greater government involvement to implement laws and practices which do not disadvantage businesses who invest in staff development but encourage them. For example, those who invest in staff education receive tax rebates. Those who do not, are taxed harder. However, first and foremost, business needs far better self-regulation. They need a new measurement standard which recognises the value of staff training/education. Businesses who invest significantly in staff education should have better long-term value creation potential and therefore attract greater investment over competitors who do not. However, as we don't have an effective, universally comparable measurement standard, to manage this facet of business, it's poorly managed. Consequently, opportunities are lost, because of our myopic and absurd profit obsession. Business is unquestionably the primary cause of this problem but by no means the only culprit.

Educational institutions have played a significant part in this problem as they have lost sight of their real purpose - to prepare students for successful working lives. Instead, they believe their role is to deliver course material successfully, irrespective of its relevance. Their measure of success is whether or not students have grasped course content, not whether business or employee find their education relevant. As they don't work closely with business, the qualifications they produce are not always relevant. They become an authority unto themselves. Consequently, their role and objectives need to change to serve business and students more effectively. In defence of educational institutions, they can do little to change things when the primary cause (business) does nothing to address the problem.

Governments also play a big part in this problem. I remember becoming alarmed when Tony Blair was Prime Minister. He believed we needed educated people, which is correct, but he and his government thought the solution was to get as many people through the university system as possible - problem solved! This just fuelled the problem of misalignment. Too many people with near useless degrees, not enough technically trained people. The clue lies in the word "misalignment." Until the three key players come together and work together in solving the problem, they will continue to act in a disjointed manner, where everybody loses, particularly employees. How would you feel - a useless degree, large debt as a result, working in an unassociated field, underpaid, with no real prospects. Frustrated, worried and upset. Not the ideal mental attitude for a workforce.

Opportunity inequality.

There are a few other factors we need to consider when looking for a better, more inclusive higher education system. While they have nothing to do with the problem of misalignment, they fall within the broader ambit of this book, and should, therefore, be taken into account.

There has been a notable decline in opportunities for people in the middle/low-income groups. Their ability to rise above the station to which they were born, has been getting more difficult. This is directly linked to increasing economic inequality. Research has proved that we can link social mobility directly to that of one's parents wealth. As real incomes have been in steady decline, so too has this adversely affected the social mobility of their offspring. Parents cannot afford to send their children to better schools or fund higher education. Further, as many can no longer afford their own homes, they are forced to live in areas of lower social standing, which negatively impacts on their social mobility.

Other concerns.

Like declining social mobility, there are other issues we need to consider when formulating plans for higher education in the future. The labour market is changing. Educational ROI (Return On Investment) is declining as more obtain the same qualification. It's becoming a crowded market with no guarantees of paying off debt incurred in obtaining a qualification. Many qualifications (for reasons already elaborated on) are of dubious value. Therefore, the risk of undertaking higher education is increasing. Also, we see the labour market polarise. Middle-class jobs are being adversely affected by computers (AI - Artificial Intelligence), mechanisation and robotics. This is forcing more people to take low-skilled work, such as "carers" and service jobs. There is also an increase in top-end high-tech jobs, but far less than are forced down the labour market. This is what is causing a polarised market. The hollowing out of mid-range jobs decreases employment opportunities, particularly for newly qualified students.

A solution - stalled.

We've identified the problem, so the solution should be obvious - get all parties to work together to produce the desired outcome. The end goal should be to have suitably trained and capable staff who are highly productive, motivated and loyal, with no personal debt. All parties benefit. Unfortunately, that's just a pipe dream. The reality is, nothing is going to change until we get the prime source of the problem - business to make fundamental changes. While outcomes are dictated by our inadequate and inappropriate measurement standard, business will continue to focus on profit creation for shareholders. Only when we have a balanced measurement standard, which accurately reflects business investment in staff development, which is an indicator and influencer of its long-term value creation potential, will businesses be encouraged to invest more in the development of staff. This will not only affect how business views education and training, but all facets influencing staff well-being. Right now this information is hidden from us, as business focuses exclusively on profit creation, at the expense of staff development and well-being (as well as other stakeholder interests.) Until then they will not accept the costs and responsibility for this important value creator. Business keeps saying, "People make the difference" and it's true, but they don't really "put their money where their mouth is." That's understandable, their hands are tied by our inadequate and inappropriate measurement standard.

Moving forward.

We have to look beyond this initial problem and believe common sense will prevail. That due to our collective efforts, particularly those of yours, in helping spread the word about the need for economic change, we will soon have a new measurement standard. Assuming we can get business to accept their responsibility for staff education/training as key driver of value creation within their business, what will this new higher education system look like?

This is no blueprint, but just my views on how a new education system of the future may best serve our needs. As soon as business accepts it's responsibility for education, which it funds, supported by the government, they will want to control the process. Key elements will be the content, its delivery and management. It will probably work much like an apprenticeship programme, where training comprises theoretical and practical training specific to an industry/sector. Students acquire theoretical training in short sessions, which are then applied practically before proceeding to the next stage, where the process is repeated. These modules will probably be short and can be mixed in any combination. Like Lego, you can build complex structures from many small building blocks. These modules will likely be developed and administered by educational institutions. Business and government should fund much of this. Government could provide subsidies/incentives to business to train their staff and impose higher taxes on those who do not. There can be no "free lunch" for businesses who think they can prosper off the back of others investment, be those competitors, other businesses or individuals.

Overhauling our education system.
The problems of our misaligned higher education will be a thing of the past when business accepts responsibility for the process. It will ensure employees are adequately trained and happy in their jobs. That educational institutions deliver what is required of them, and government steps up to the mark and helps fund the process. Government needs to put in place the checks and balances to ensure the interests of the majority are served. This will include a provision to ensure equality of access to jobs and training for all. Further, individuals will no longer be burdened by educational debt.

The purpose of our education and training is to equip us to excel in the workplace. Businesses will want education/training to be specific to their industry/sector rather than generic. To this end, they would work closely with educational institutions to find out how to deliver both theoretical and practical programmes which will optimise staff performance. This should not be too narrow as to blinker people as to wider possibilities.

Ideally, people should enter the higher education system through work placement. After a relatively short period of industry/sector orientation, giving people "on the job" time to learn more about whether the career is for them before launching their education. The employee would then enter an appropriate branch of education with a specific industry bias to meet both their and their employee's needs. Business becomes the education hub, supported by educational institutions, who may deliver, and manage the employee's progress. Business sponsors their staff on their education/training journey. The education system must become flexible and adaptable to business and market needs, delivering appropriate training to meet the challenges facing the industry/sector.

Universities, rather than provide degree courses, should offer a selection of smaller mix and match courses, designed around industry/sector needs, made available through industry bodies and delivered mainly online. Emphasis will be on their practical application. Learning will, therefore, shift back to the workplace. So, universities will become centres for the delivery and management of higher education, not of learning. I see the future role of universities not as teaching institutions - others can teach what we already know, but to lead in what we don't know. I see their primary role as becoming centres of excellence for R&D. Other educational institutions who provide more technically based courses, which require hands-on training may provide training centres for this purpose. Otherwise, they work like any other of the business's training/educational programmes.

So, rather than acquiring a generic qualification, people will earn learning credits as they progress. This is similar to the CPD (Continuous Professional Development) scheme used in the UK, where points are allocated for specific activities. Rather than seeing education/training end with a formal qualification, this method encourages ongoing education and should include all staff members.

The end of an era.

Going to university to acquire a general degree in a particular field should become a thing of the past. In the near future, people will enter the workplace and be sponsored by their business to undertake further education/training, specific to their industry/sector. This will be the start of them building their CPD portfolio. Educational institutions will be responsive and adaptable to industry/sector needs by providing appropriate and valuable educational material and support, to enhance staff productivity and value. Some of the educational material may be applicable across many sectors, so not all components will be unique to an industry and sector, but how they construct and implement such programmes will be. Education becomes tailor made not generic, using small building blocks to achieve this.

People will only follow a specific training direction once they have shown a desire to do so and an understanding of what's involved, together with business approval, as both parties will benefit. The type and construction of courses will vary in length and content, but will always be grounded in business needs (because that's where we apply our knowledge, understanding and skills.) Education must be an integral part of business, not some remote, independent process, constructed and implemented by those not close enough to business to fully understand their needs. Education must become an extension of the business, so, independent educational institutions can't possibly know what's best for business. Educational institutions can and must contribute to the process, but cannot set the curriculum independently of business. Their goals and those of business must fully align.

Individuals can still fund their own courses, through an industry/sector body. They may do so to show their keenness to enter an industry/sector, but this expenditure would need to be reimbursed by the business should they be fortunate to enter the industry. The business, in turn, should be able to claim back on government rebates. This is to ensure a fair labour market. It eliminates the possibility of business shifting educational funding back onto individuals, or others, and ending up with poorly educated/trained individuals. By businesses reimbursing individuals for courses privately funded, eliminates, to a certain degree, the advantage of those who could fund better university education (i.e. it neutralises opportunity inequality.)

Using the Lego approach (comprising small building blocks) in education allows one to create precisely what's required, rather than use a pre-designed, inappropriate, or less appropriate course. The analogy of using a sledgehammer to crack a nut is appropriate, except business expects the individual to pay for the sledgehammer. This new approach is tailored to an employer, and their employee's on the job needs. Each small building block goes towards building the employers CPD portfolio or log. A highly educated/trained individual would have a CPD portfolio with a high score. This would also include work experience gained from exposure rather than training. In expressing these views, I'm not implying that individuals cannot shape their own education beyond the confines of their immediate work requirement. They should be able to fund their own education. Forward thinking and capable individuals are those who recognise education as a never-ending process. If the business does not wish to fund their endeavours, then individuals can go ahead and do it on their own. Business would only be responsible for "foundation" qualification but could fund further advanced courses if there is a business case for it.

Education and training is an ongoing process, which the CPD log will reflect. A CPD log is dynamic in the sense that it can contract as well as expand. If I consider my career as an example, in the mid-'70s and early 80's I was proficient in most of the popular computer programming languages, such as Cobol, Fortran, Basic, and a few others. These would have added nicely to my CPD log at the time, but to leave them on today would overstate my real value. Fortunately, I have replaced them with more current online systems like MySql, PHP, HTML, CSS and javascript. There are many other things I have done in business over the past forty years which are no longer particularly relevant. Expertise and knowledge in bygone practices have to be adjusted for. In some cases, they will be valueless, in others their value will be significantly reduced, while in others, they can be a liability. Those trained to think and act in an outdated way are a liability, not an asset. Think of the many business, and political leaders taught, and/or conditioned to believe in outdated beliefs, such as free markets and globalisation (i.e. liberal economies.) Their "experience" and "knowledge" is a liability to many, in our modern world.

So, a CPD log should be a reflection of how relevant and valuable we are now, not an accumulation of irrelevant knowledge. Consequently, it should encourage on-going commitment by individuals and business to the acquisition of relevant knowledge and removal of outdated and inhibiting practices.

In closing this chapter, let's not forget all I've said about making business the hub of education supported by educational institutions and government will not happen until we change our inadequate and inappropriate business measurement standard. To be brutally honest, all I've been doing is paying lip service to the value of education. This is because without fundamental change to our business measurement standard nothing changes. It's all just hot air. The reality is our current measurement standard inhibits change by focusing on, and demanding the optimisation of short-term profits. Until our measurement standard is replaced by a fully inclusive value creation standard, which understands and accounts for the value created through training/education, adequate investment in education is a wild unattainable dream. We will continue to march backwards.

Summary.
We've all heard the saying "People make the difference," and most of us believe it to be true. It's because people run businesses, which provides the foundation for this truth. They perform most tasks and make most decisions, which affect those who deal with them. People create great experiences and value for money, which we all want. People are creative and come up with innovative ideas. Therefore, it's people who make the difference between our good and bad experiences. As obvious as this is and as obvious

the link is between education/training and customer satisfaction, business continues to under invest significantly in this most critical facet. Why, because, we've set up our systems to optimise short-term profit to serve the needs of shareholders and other vested interests, without regard to other stakeholders.

Many know our broken education system does not deliver what's needed, but they can do little about it because our economic systems prevent change from happening. Consequently, business through its lack of adequate funding has shifted its responsibilities onto others so business can optimise short-term profits. This has meant individuals provide the funding, while others who are not particularly close to the needs of business design, develop and implement education/training programmes. The result – huge personal debt, misaligned education, poorly equipped staff and therefore underperforming economies. We will only solve this problem when we remove our self-serving economic systems, most notably our inadequate and inappropriate business measurement standard.

Chapter 11
New epoch – new rules.

You've made it this far - to the final chapter. If there is one resounding message the book has left you with, I hope it's an appreciation of the depth and breadth of the manipulation of our economy by a wealthy few. The economy should serve the needs of you and I, those who make up ninety-nine per cent of the population, but it doesn't. The course of democracy has been perverted by the wealthy and powerful to serve them, not us. This is not good for either the wealthy or poor, as it represents injustice, and injustice is a time bomb. It is this point which leads me onto the subject matter of this final chapter. If we continue as we are, socially, environmentally and economically, we are soon to reach a tipping point. Like the proverbial last straw on the camel's back. My concern is that in the near future we face major, game-changing technologies. These changes are not light like straw, but huge, heavy concrete blocks. They will definitely break the camels back. If we don't change our economic systems now, to serve the majority, what impact will our self-serving economy have on new game-changing technologies when introduced? We have seen the damaging effects their economic manipulations inflict on society and the environment. If we give business free reign (as they want) over these new technologies without the guiding and protecting hand of government, I fear the worse. If self-interest and greed are to decide the direction these new technologies follow, they will inflict massive damage. The bigger the change, the bigger its impact, and we face enormous change. The problem is, we haven't much time before these new technologies become everyday realities. This chapter explains the impact these new technologies will have on our lives and why we need new economic systems to usher them in.

The "gig" economy -
a harbinger of worsening worker rights.

To emphasise my point of how business seizes upon relatively small market changes to manipulate them for shareholder's benefit at the expense of stakeholders, take the "gig" economy as an example. Business knows it may take years (if at all) for legislation to catch up and rectify their exploitative practices.

Where small governments exist and free markets dominate, it's unlikely any intervention will take place. Governments are often far behind the curve of change, only responding when problems become intolerable. Consider how far behind regulation is for social media. It stands accused of producing "Fake News" and spreading harmful and inciteful material, whose content undermines the fabric of society and democracy. With this new epoch, governments need to be close to the change curve. Otherwise, the extent of change will swamp even the biggest government. Changes which have led to the rise of the "gig" economy are small in comparison to the changes we face - yet they caught us offside for years. Imagine when the rate and extent of change is so much greater, we won't cope, unless we are close to these changes. However, no government, even big government can be up-to-date with the latest changes, because that's not their role. Businesses innovate, not governments. They will always lag behind. So, the only way to keep business in check, as best as possible, is through better self-regulation, using a new measurement standard which considers all stakeholder interests. This together with the introduction of *Inclusive Theory*, which involves consumers becoming more responsible for the products/services they use, will stop, or slow the introduction of poor practices, not in the interest of the common good. This would allow regulation to catch up much quicker (i.e. put government closer to the curve.)

Consider how the "gig" economy subtly, but radically changed business labour practices, treating workers who carry out vital tasks for the business as self-employed individuals. This enabled these businesses to reduce their risk and costs by shifting the financial burden onto their workers. They reduced their costs by not paying overtime, downtime, sick leave or holiday pay. Neither do they contribute to pensions, unemployment insurance and in some cases health insurance. By reducing their costs, they are more profitable and less susceptible to the risk of downturns. These businesses have shifted all these costs and risks onto their workers, who are generally "people of straw" - ill-equipped to bear such costs and risks.

This form of labour contract is nothing other than exploitation. Workers, irrespective of their employment status should be given basic rights of protection. What society are we, where we allow businesses to exploit people in this way? I understand some people want flexible working conditions, but there is a clear distinction between flexibility and exploitation. Businesses who provide flexible working conditions must also provide proportionate rights and pay for them. These businesses have tried to gain a competitive advantage through their "disruptive" business model at the expense of worker rights. Workers and competitors are not the only ones to suffer. Most suffer because governments lose tax revenues and have to pick up the social costs of these unfair and immoral practices. Eventually, we all pay for these costs through higher taxes, which these "disrupter" businesses profited unfairly from.

Zero hour contracts are almost as bad as "gig" economy practices. Zero hour contracts provide some worker protection, but not enough. What about unpaid internships, another popular practice? These are all forms of exploitation. Together, they are the harbinger of how business uses change to increase their wealth, without a second thought for their worker's well-being. We don't live in a world of "enlightenment" where we see the interests of our fellow human beings as important - as influencing our well-being. We live in a world of self-interest and greed, so we need to protect ourselves from these self-interests.

Even relatively small changes, like the "gig economy" allow businesses the opportunity to slip through new practices for their shareholder's benefit, as that is what they see as their purpose. As already mentioned, business is at the leading edge of change, and that change brings the opportunity of doing things differently. Government is often too far behind these changes to take quick action (if necessary), therefore we need better self-regulation in the form of business measures and for consumers to play their part as an effective watchdog. Based on our current standard of using a financial measure to assess business performance, we would applaud the "gig" economy as being a highly profitable model. However, a balanced measurement standard would immediately have identified worker exploitation as a problem area and tagged it. A balanced measurement standard is a means of putting us at the leading edge of change, as it gauges change across the entire business, not just financial impact.

If change is big and extensive, then without the right measures in place, it will overwhelm us, bringing misery and hardship to the majority. However, with the proper systems in place, I'm optimistic and excited about the benefits it should bring all. I will now explain the changes we are likely to face - they are life-changing. It's the type of change which introduces a new epoch.

New technologies.
Much of the recent productivity gains enjoyed in the manufacturing sector have been achieved through robotics. Their extensive use has been hidden from us behind factory doors. So, robotics have been with us for some time. That is not to say they won't continue to grow rapidly, finding new areas of application. In fact, robotics and mechanisation will continue to improve manufacturing productivity by eliminating labour or enhancing its usage. Either way, it will lead to a smaller workforce. The use of robotics and mechanisation within manufacturing is an obvious area of application. What we are not too clear on at this stage is the impact AI (Artificial Intelligence) will have on the labour market, in all market sectors. AI is relatively new compared to robotics and mechanisation, but I believe it will have as big, or even bigger impact.

My concern, which is the subject of this chapter, is that we face a double whammy in the labour market, which if not addressed now, presents us with a potentially dire situation. On the one hand, business's reliance on labour in the near future will be vastly reduced. On the other hand, we face a rapidly increasing population. Therefore, mass unemployment throughout the world, with all its associated problems, is a strong probability. Unless our economic systems are changed to serve the many, the current system, designed to serve the needs of a few, will probably lead to anarchy. Our current system pays no regard to the plight of the average citizen. It continues to exploit opportunities to optimise profits for shareholders, at the expense of all others, because, that's what its designed to do. Robotics and AI will provide increased opportunity to eliminate labour and increase profits further. The rich will get considerably richer while the poor miserably poorer. The masses will quickly become disillusioned and rebel, possibly violently. This will be a gargantuan screw-up. If we resist the opportunities to change now, it will lead to a new order – whatever that may be. Vested interests will be one of the many losers, so they should heed the signs. For once, they should look a little further than quarterly earnings, to protect their long-term interests. Let's make the transition to a more inclusive economy where all can enjoy a better life while also protecting the environment. Robotics and AI represent a new epoch – we need new systems and rules to ensure this epoch serves all.

Diminishing labour contribution.

Robotics and mechanisation play a major role in reducing our reliance on labour. We can produce more, at a lower cost of consistent, and often higher quality. Its widespread adoption will soon reduce the biased advantages low labour cost countries have over developed economies. This is an important reason not to lose manufacturing capabilities (as already explained) for short-term labour cost savings (encouraged by free markets.) This advance in technology means that irrespective of where a product is produced, labour input will decline dramatically, and this is of concern. Developed economies have already felt the pinch as manufacturing has left their shores for low labour cost production elsewhere, increasing their unemployment rates and social problems. Low labour cost countries will soon feel the effects of labour loss, but at least they will retain their manufacturing base, with all its positive effects.

The AI epoch.

Robotics and mechanisation has had a major impact on manufacturing and will continue to develop rapidly. However, I'm of the opinion that the biggest change will be felt through AI. It won't just replace certain jobs but will pervade the entire workforce by providing some form of assistance to dramatically increase productivity, thereby reducing the overall workforce. I would like to draw on an analogy between my early days as a computer programmer and how AI will change most jobs. In my early days, way back in the early 70's, I started programming in machine code. It's complex because you have to manage all aspects of the computer. Then clever developers started introducing higher level languages which relieved programmers of all the drudgery of machine code. Programmers productivity increased hugely through these so called "high level languages." The same is true for the early days of on-line computing. It used to be a field for specialists until some clever people started producing tools and applications which increased productivity hugely. These new tools have made it so simple even non-technical people can develop their own on-line bespoke systems relatively easily.

The same will happen to most, if not all jobs, where they will be simplified by systems and apps, driven by some underlying AI. We see it all around us. If it hasn't already started to affect you it soon will. Workers carry "intelligent devices" with them which they use to do their job or paperwork quicker. There are literally hundreds of thousands of applications for specific jobs – an app for everything, and this is only the beginning. So it won't necessarily be a matter of a direct threat from AI to replace your job, but rather AI taking away much of the drudgery of work, improving productivity significantly. This means a reduction in the workforce, just as automation and robotics removed drudgery, doing a better and faster job of it. The increase in "productivity tools" and industry/sector specific software will increase job losses.

Every job will be affected – it's just the degree of influence which is different. Some may not be affected that badly while others may be completely replaced. News reports and articles place their emphasis on those jobs which are likely to be replaced, or significantly affected. This gives people a false sense of security - "at least I'm not on that list", but that's not the reality of the situation. All jobs will be affected and this will result in an overall reduction in our reliance on labour. Every job will require less labour input. There will be an increase in jobs requiring creative input, but again, these jobs will be assisted by productivity tools.

The more repetitive a job, with little or no creative input, are obvious targets for replacement. Strange as it may seem, highly technical jobs with multiple, complex inputs and thus complex decisions are also at high risk because these tasks are better suited to huge "number crunchers" with access to massive databases and effective AI. Medical diagnosis is one such area. Roles may change where less well trained individuals (i.e. those with less recall to knowledge) act as the human go-betweens in a medical consultation conducted by AI. The legal and engineering professions are equally attractive to AI developers. Your job is at threat in some way or other. Things are going to change radically, and machines are going to be able to make better, more accurate and complex decisions than humans. We will have driverless vehicles travelling faster, with fewer accidents. We will have autonomous deliveries. Products will be produced, stored, delivered to customers and off-loaded with no human intervention. Retail stores will be packed autonomously according to up-to-the-minute sales data. Shelf pricing will be automated. You will select products from the store and walkout without passing through tills. Costs for your purchases will be automatically debited to your account. This isn't mad hatter, futuristic gobbledygook, but technologies being worked on and perfected right now.

A glance into the future.
I worked in the FMCG (Fast Moving Consumer Goods) sector, (which is a major contributor to the economy) in executive positions for many years, with responsibilities for manufacturing, distribution and retailing. If I interpret the technological developments I have seen and expect, some of which I mentioned above, I foresee massive job losses throughout the entire supply chain. The anticipated losses experienced in this sector will be mirrored across numerous other sectors. Let's have a look at the jobs by department to see how extensively they will be affected.

A. Raw material stores.
Goods will be received by autonomous delivery. They are checked in by AI, with all necessary sampling conducted autonomously before being packed away by automated handling equipment. All

documentation and accounting is done electronically. No human input is required.

Materials are drawn automatically and delivered to the point of production with all relevant documentation updated by a fully integrated computer system. Again, no people input required.

B. Production.

Already most of the production in this sector is mechanised. The few remaining labour roles will soon be replaced by robotics as the processes are repetitive and therefore ideally suited to robotics. Quality control is possibly one of those jobs at risk. If not replaced by technology, they will certainly be highly affected by robotics, mechanisation and AI, requiring fewer quality controllers, or less skilled controllers. The factory floor of the future will have very few if any people on it. Thirty years ago its was abuzz with people.

C. Product stores.

As with raw material stores, finished product stores will be packed, monitored and efficiently managed through mechanisation, robotics and AI. There will be no need for people.

D. Distribution.

Picking and packing of orders in the most cost effective way will be automated, including all stock accounting and billing information. Delivery to customer's warehouse or store will be done by driverless vehicles. Off loading is automated as well. No people required here either.

In the case of all four departments I said "no people required." This isn't all together true, because, people will be in the background monitoring the automation, ensuring all is running smoothly. After all, these are only machines programmed to do specific processes. If something unforeseen happens, real intelligence has to step in and rectify the problems. Unfortunately, only one overseer is required for every hundred, or perhaps thousands of jobs lost. However, the development of the conscious computers may replace the overseer in the near future.

E Retailing.
Back-room stock.
Stock is delivered autonomously and packed in the back-room store. No people required. No documentation - all is electronically transferred and verified at store, including the scanning for damaged stock.

Store packing/merchandising.
Both these functions are carried out by robots. Shelf pricing is automated using electronic displays. No people required.

Checkouts.
There will be no checkouts in the future. A number of different scenarios are being investigated at the moment to replace checkouts for the convenience of the shopper and to reduce the cost of cashiers. Whatever direction this follows, the outcome is the same – no checkouts; no cashiers. Ideas being considered are using apps on mobile devices to scan products and automatically debit accounts. Scanning an entire basket in micro-seconds, with automatic payments. Using payment apps and proximity tabs to link the product to a device when the product is moved and is in close proximity to a devise. The product is automatically placed on the devices "shopping tab" and when the device leaves the store the account linked to the device is automatically debited.

These changes mean store's won't even have managers. They will have system overseers with responsibility to ensure the machines are functioning correctly. So, not all human jobs will be lost, but for every overseer, hundreds of jobs will go. In fact, at every stage throughout the supply chain, managerial roles will also be lost. We don't need them any more.

F. Sales.
With advancing AI and access to up-to-date supplier pricing and volume discounts, together with store sales data, computer to computer trading is a reality, possibly replacing the manufacturer's salespeople. It will certainly reduce the size of their sales team no matter what. We have computers trading with computers on the stock exchange, accounting for a large portion of trades. This form of trading will rapidly move into new markets

as there is a labour saving, and purchasing efficiencies (as purchasing is driven by greater data insight, analysed with the help of AI.)

G. Marketing.

Marketing still requires a certain degree of creativity (not that it's apparent, considering much of the advertising and promotional activity currently in the market.) AI can assist in this creative process by generating ideas, or by gathering content. Such productivity tools are already freely available. "Big Data" - the acquisition and analysis of vast amounts of information to assist in profiling and preparing targeted messages is growing rapidly. Marketers can do more with fewer people and this trend will accelerate.

The potential loss of jobs in this sector alone is frightening. It's not going to happen immediately, but it will happen soon enough. This loss will be mirrored in other sectors. The application of similar technologies across the broad spectrum of business will require little tweaking.

The downside.

Vested interests may become excited at the prospect of eliminating or reducing labour costs and replacing them with these new technologies. The prospect of increased productivity and quality is enticing. It spells higher profits. However, there is a major downside to these new technologies. Robots, machines and computers don't buy many things apart from the occasional spare part and regular service. The loss of income by many millions around the world means there won't be too much work for the machines either. Economies need a strong middle class. It is this simple fact which vested interests will overlook in their haste to use technology for their own ends. Wiping out the income base of multiple-millions will be disastrous for national economies and therefore the global economy.

A question for you.

Given the potential massive job losses we face, affecting every job from those at the "coalface", throughout management, including the threat to many highly technical jobs, together with the socio-economic ramifications of this, here's a question for you. What type of economic environment do you want to oversee and manage the introduction of these new technologies? Do you want our current, self-centred, profiteering economic system which serves only the needs of an elite rich to oversee this new epoch. They have already wreaked enough economic, social and environmental havoc with their self-serving systems. These new technologies will enable them to enrich themselves at a far greater rate in the future, at the expense of those who will lose their jobs and cannot find new careers. In a previous chapter we have considered the effects of labour polarisation, which will get worse, quicker. The likelihood that this new epoch will affect you and your family is high, because, its impact will be so widespread.

Or, would you prefer that these new technologies to be introduced into an economic system which is in balance. An economic system which considers what's best for all, and manages change accordingly. To have the process overseen by big government, which is capable of imposing regulation which serves all, after carefully considering the ramifications on what serves the common good best.

I'm not calling for these new technologies to be stopped - far from it, but to ensure they are not introduced into an economic environment solely interested in the short-term enrichment of a few, at the expense of all others. That will be the biggest disaster we have ever faced. This new epoch requires new rules. We need to make the changes to our economic systems now, not later. These technologies are on our doorstep, you already feel their presence, and seen the results. We don't have much time to change. Please support the calls for change and spread the word far and wide as often as you can.

Summary.

We are facing game-changing technologies. The reason it's a game-changer is that it will affect everybody's role in the economy. Change so big, it's capable of replacing you entirely or increasing productivity so much that we require fewer people. Your job - your income, in the future will be at risk, this is a certainty. The same applies to your entire family and friends. How will you live?

You have a choice - how do you want these new technologies introduced - under the guidance and control of vested interests who put profit before all else? Alternatively, do you want it introduced under better economic systems, which consider the needs of all, backed by big government, which will ensure we meet society needs first?

If like most others you opt for the latter, then you have also accepted responsibility to spread the word so that we can implement change. If you just nod your head in agreement, nothing changes. Vested interest wins the war. We fight and win through numbers. We have the numbers, provided we all play our part. It may be a small part, but a valuable part nonetheless. All you have to do is start by spreading the word as far and as wide as you can, as often as you can. That's how you secure your future and that of your family.

Conclusion and observations

Conclusion

This book ends with the words *THE BEGINNING.*
It's only the first step in a long journey.
As a first step it has (hopefully) made you aware of the source of our economic problems and made it clear that these are man-made problems, which we can overturn. Our political system has been working to increase inequality and reduce the quality of opportunity. This isn't how a democracy is supposed to work, but that's how it's working, and we need to change it. Inequality is not a problem of redistribution, but of bad economic management through bad systems. Poor quality of opportunity is a direct result of increasing economic inequality. Inequality also lowers productivity, efficiency and beneficial growth. It causes increased instability, both economically and socially, and introduces greater hardship for the majority. We experience economic growth, but only a few benefit from it. That's not how it should work.

Armed with this understanding, the next step is for you to spread the word as far and wide as possible. Use your social networks to do this. As a single voice, we have no chance of bringing about change, facing such a powerful, influential and determined opponent. Stakes are high, so, they won't take any challenge lying down. However, facing a multitude of disenchanted and disgruntled citizens, fed up with the devious manipulations of our economic systems, can, through force of numbers, sway public and political opinion, and be no match for them.

The third step is to keep the pressure up demanding change. A single battle won't win this war. Continuous pressure is how our opponents changed systems, procedures, practices and laws to serve them and work against us. We now need to apply the same methods against them. Ask your MP what they are doing about these problems. Write to the media and ask them the same question. Ask associations and institutions who represent different facets of business what they are doing. You may already belong to one or more of them.

You are fighting for a fairer and sustainable future for yourself and your family – so the effort is well worth it. Theresa May made this comment before a no-confidence vote in her leadership in December 2018, "We need to work towards a stronger economy, as that's what the people want." That's only part of "what the people want." People want the economy to work for them, not others. First, make sure the economy works for the majority, and then grow it. There is no point in growing an economy whose growth will hurt the majority. Our political class have a long way to go in getting the fundamentals right.

The Internet has given power to public opinion, which we need to use "to level the playing field" (pardon the hackneyed cliche) in getting our message out and sustaining it, just as vested interests have done in influencing the message over the past forty years.

Good luck!

Observations

Below are some interesting observations made by some super-rich individuals about our economic inequality.

From within the inner sanctum.

From within the hallowed inner sanctum of the super-rich, a young quivering voice was heard. It was way back in 2006 when it was first heard. It belonged to Jamie Johnson, heir apparent to the Johnson & Johnson empire. He was voicing his concern about economic inequality, but alas, heard from no more. Oh - surprise, surprise.

Jamie made a film titled "The One Per Cent" (which is available on You Tube), where he highlights the numerous problems associated with the widening gap between rich and poor. He was concerned about the problems this inequality causes and used his privileged position to try and find some answers. His family and others were reluctant to answer questions and it was suggested he just leave things as they are. He has done so, so have they. To say nothing has changed since then would be wrong - problems have worsened.

In an interview with Forbes in February 2008, he was asked (among other questions) the following:-

"Question: **So what's your solution? What do you propose we do about this growing disparity?**
That's a great question. One of the interesting things that happened along this journey for me was that I thought that Ph.D.s and the specialists I interviewed on the subject would have specific answers and they'd say this is what we need to do to solve the problem. But they didn't. It's an incredibly messy subject. The most interesting answers? Some people would say, "Listen, we need to tax the rich more than we are. They're getting richer and richer and they're pulling away from the rest of society, isolating themselves and creating this tension between classes." They'd also say, "We need to provide better social services. We need things like higher standards for education and higher standards for health care. Those are things that help a society grow and help a middle class grow, which is what we need more of in this country."

Question: **You'll have people like Milton Friedman, who you've included in the film, who will argue there's nothing wrong with this accumulation of wealth; that it's a product of capitalism. What do you say to that?**
Interestingly, Milton Friedman did say that the growing wealth gap was bad for society.

Question: **Sure, the gap itself, but perhaps not that accumulation of wealth.**
He has a different solution for the problem. He believes what you have to do is cut taxes, take regulation out of the economy and allow families like mine to accumulate as much wealth as they possibly can so that it can trickle down into the hands of people in the middle and lower classes."

Of course Jamie did not uncover any solutions - the so called specialists (lackeys of the wealthy one per cent, to whom he belongs,) aren't looking for them. They don't want to pull down what they have so carefully built up over the decades. All the things which serve their needs. What sort of answer would one expect to receive from Milton Friedman (now deceased,) the "father" of free market economics - nothing but the same old drivel fed to us ad nauseam over the past forty years. His thinking has been at the heart of our problems.

Strangely enough, in 2014 another voice was heard from within the inner sanctum. In August 2014, Politico Magazine (politico.com) published an article by Nick Hanauer, an American billionaire, titled "The Pitchforks Are Coming For Us Plutocrats". In the article he talks about the problems economic inequality will cause people like himself - members of the wealthy one per cent. Part of what he had to say was, "The problem isn't that we have inequality. Some inequality is intrinsic to any high-functioning capitalist economy. The problem is that inequality is at historically high levels and getting worse every day. Our country is rapidly becoming less a capitalist society and more a feudal society. Unless our policies change dramatically, the middle class will disappear, and we will be back to late 18th-century France. Before the revolution. And so I have a message for my fellow filthy rich, for all of us who live in our gated bubble worlds: Wake up, people. It won't last.

If we don't do something to fix the glaring inequities in this economy, the pitchforks are going to come for us. No society can sustain this kind of rising inequality. In fact, there is no example in human history where wealth accumulated like this and the pitchforks didn't eventually come out. You show me a highly unequal society, and I will show you a police state. Or an uprising. There are no counterexamples. None. It's not if, it's when."

Resisting change.
Nick is right, but it's many years since he spoke out and nothing has changed, and unlikely to. It's getting worse. Jamie Johnson in his interview with Forbes highlighted the abject lack of thought leadership in this field. I know it's not due to inability, it's just that they don't want change and aren't looking for solutions (as highlighted in Chapter One.)

Over the years, my work in looking for solutions to our measurement standard problems brought me into contact with people from the accounting profession, mainly academics, bodies representing the profession and leading practitioners. In dealing with one of the leading professional bodies, I challenged them on fundamental issues regarding creating value for all stakeholders. I was informed by one of my contacts that he could no longer be in discussion with me as I was "rocking the boat" to violently. It was not worth his job or pension to continue, although he saw merit in what I was saying. This sums it up, "Don't rock the boat." It's okay to create small waves, but definitely not big ones. Unfortunately for them, we need a tsunami. When they have dissenters, they batten down and block them out. It's the wrong approach to bury your head in the sand, but then they think there's no looming threat, or need for change. They've hidden the problem successfully for so long, why worry now? How wrong they are.

I faced the same problem when approaching the relevant department in the UK government (Department for Business, Energy and Industrial Strategy) about the need for a new measurement standard. Their abject lack of understanding and appreciation of the problem was breath-taking. I don't blame them entirely, they cannot be knowledgeable in all matters, and rely on "expert opinion." Unfortunately, their experts are those I referred to in Chapter One, who are supposed to be looking for a "solution" and yet are incapable of even identifying our minimum requirements for a solution. What type of expert is that?

You are change.
We cannot expect change to come from within – anywhere from within. Even the possibility of a violent uprising does nothing to persuade them. They are onto something too good to relinquish. Responsibility for change lies with us. We know the problems, we know what the solutions look like, we must now take action. Collectively we are a force to be reckoned with. Start spreading the news now.

Appendix A

Standard-of-living and quality-of-life.

Throughout this book, I have referred to two measures – standard-of-living and quality-of-life. I told you that vested interest has conflated these two terms to hide the fact that while standard-of-living is rising, quality-of-life is falling rapidly. While both measures are important, quality-of-life has a greater impact on life. We need to be clear on what these terms mean and who is responsible for them.

Standard-of-living.

Neither standard-of-living nor quality-of-life is measured effectively, yet they are the two most important social indicators we have. They, together with an environmental index, would provide a good understanding of our well being; a far better indicator than our almost worthless GDP measure. Despite their desirability, we don't measure them because they don't serve vested interests needs. In fact, they would work against their interests. They would have to forego wealth/value as it would be more evenly distributed among the majority, while also protecting our environment. This shows the importance of measures; they dictate outcomes. You use measures to achieve the outcomes you want. That's why the wealthy one per cent dictate measurement standards for both micro and macroeconomic measures.

Standard-of-living refers to products and services made available to citizens of a particular country. If we did measure it, the best method would be to use a "basket" of products similar to the basket idea used in calculating Retail Price Index (RPI, used to gauge inflation.) Obviously, the products in the "basket" are entirely different and are representative of what the average person uses in their life. They represent products and services which are affordable; within the financial reach of the average citizen, and in general use. The basket is divided into categories, which are then subdivided into sub-categories. Within these sub-categories, the products and services comprising the sub-category are listed. Each product/service is scored by its availability and affordability. If it's readily available it scores highly and if it's easily affordable it scores highly. These are combined to give an overall score. The product/service is then weighted by its importance within the subcategory and a final score calculated. Scores are then aggregated, and a final index score is determined. (This describes the principle of the index in broad terms only.) The categories comprising the index are

- Home,
- Food,
- Clothing,
- Travel,
- Entertainment,
- Communication.

As you have gathered, standard-of-living is influenced by business. They are responsible for introducing new products into categories, improving them and lowering their costs, making them more affordable and readily available. This, in turn, improves the standard-of-living index. The higher the index, the better. Government plays an important part in creating the favourable and supportive environment which allows all this to happen. It plays an important part in ensuring product/services are provided in a competitive environment, otherwise prices would rise and standard-of-living drop. However, having said that, it's the entrepreneurial flair behind business which "delivers the goodies" at a price we can afford.

Quality-of-life.

Quality-of-life deals with the different aspects which directly affect how we live our lives. These different aspects are determined by the government who formulates policies and implement laws, procedures and practices to regulate the context in which we live, to benefit its citizens. It includes such things as:-

- Work   Availability, security, conditions, wages.
- Housing   Availability, affordability, security.
- Health   Availability, affordability, standard.
- Security   Availability, standard.
- Finance   Individual levels of debt/savings
- Education   Availability, affordability, standard.
- Transport   Availability, affordability, standard,
  congestion

- Amenities   Availability, standard.
- Environment   Pollution - air, water, land, noise,
                availability of open spaces.

Quality-of-life is also not measured officially. It's calculated as an index by measuring categories and sub-categories, to determine the individual and overall direction of the index. What is happening here in the UK is mirrored across most, if not all, developed economies. In the UK, we are facing a significant decline in quality-of-life, as reflected below. The actual indices are not shown, but rather relative movements over the past decade.

Work	Availability	Stagnant/ In decline.
	Security	In decline (threat of new technologies.)
	Conditions	In decline (workers rights.)
	Wages	In decline (in real terms.)
Housing	Availability	In decline.
	Affordability	In decline
	Security	In decline (higher percentage renters.)
Health	Availability	In decline (NHS under extreme pressure.)
	Affordability	In decline (UK citizens resorting to private healthcare.)
	Standard	In decline (NHS under extreme pressure.)
Security	Availability	In decline (Policing cut backs.)
	Standard	In decline (Policing cut backs.)
Finance	Level of debt	Increasing.
	Level of saving	In decline.
Education	Availability	In decline. (Budget cuts reducing available options.)
	Affordability	In decline.(Individuals must fund previously available options now unavailable due to austerity.)
	Standard	In decline.
Transport	Availability	In decline. (The standard of public transport is declining.)

	Affordability	In decline. (Rising with inflation, but salaries don't.)
	Standard	In decline. (Old infrastructure.)
	Congestion	Worsening. (Old infrastructure – greater number of users.)
Amenities	Availability	In decline. (Victim of extended austerity programmes.)
	Standard	In decline. (If services remain, they have been cutback.)
Environment	Protection	In decline.
	Regeneration	Stagnant/In decline.

The above paints rather a bleak picture. No wonder there is such public unease and discontent. Now you can understand why vested interests want to conflate these two measures. The one (standard-of-living) is doing well because it's in the one per cent's direct interests to keep improving products and services which lead to an improved standard-of-living. However, what's needed to build quality-of-life - big government and decent tax margins are precisely what vested interests don't want. They get their way, and as a result, quality-of-life is in rapid decline, yet its quality-of-life which affects life more profoundly.

Appendix B

Why is our measurement standard inadequate and inappropriate?

Throughout the book, I have been saying that our business measurement standard is inadequate and inappropriate and the root cause of some of our most serious social, environmental, economic and business problems. Therefore, it's important we look at the reasons why in a little more detail. If we can make only one change to our economic systems, then it must be to change our measurement standard. Remember, if you want to control outcomes, then control the measures, as measures dictate outcomes. That's why the wealthy one per cent control both microeconomic and macroeconomic measures.

Business represents the foundation block of our economy. What we do in business dictates what we do in our economy. The most important thing affecting every business is how we measure it. It affects operational, tactical and strategic decisions every day. There is nothing which has a more profound effect on outcomes than its measures. As the old adage goes, "What you measure is what you get," shows to what extent measures affect outcomes. Therefore, it's critically important that our measurement standard aligns with our social and business objectives of sustained, long-term value creation for all. Instead, what we have now is a measurement standard which aligns with the needs of shareholders, to the exclusion of all others. Because of this fundamental misalignment, we should not be surprised at the mess our economy is in.

Our Accounting Model is a financial measurement standard. As a financial measure it's good, but as a business measure, it's inadequate and inappropriate, because financial considerations only make up a small percentage of business decisions. It's inappropriate use as a business measure lies at the heart of our problems. We need a more balanced perspective, which considers the needs of all contributors to business, as they all affect the well-being of business, not just financial capital.

There are seven main reasons why the Accounting Model does not provide the correct measurement framework for measuring and managing long-term value creation for all, and they are: -

1. It does not provide the correct measurement base.

Most see profit as being exclusively and inextricably linked with the Accounting Model. Few question the Accounting Model's validity or appropriateness in driving the profit objective. We take it for granted; we do not question or challenge it. However, are these assumptions correct? Can we only achieve the profit objective by adopting a financial perspective? This is definitely not true! Only when you query the appropriateness of the Accounting Model are we led, quickly, to some startling facts, such as:-

a. You can only use the Accounting Model to measure a few business processes; the vast bulk of business processes are excluded from measurement. What proportion is excluded? This is difficult to answer with any degree of accuracy. As a "rule of thumb", research suggests Book Value (i.e. the value ascribed to the business by the Accounting Model) only represents about 20% of Market Value (i.e. the value ascribed to the business by its shareholders) to infer that the Accounting Model only measures a similar number of business processes. So, as a rough guide, or rule of thumb, we can conclude the Accounting Model excludes approximately 80% of our business processes from measurement. In other words, it's a highly exclusive measurement standard: inappropriate as a business measure.

b. The question we now need to ask ourselves is, "Do the business processes, which are excluded from measurement, add value?" I'll answer this with another question, "Why undertake a business process that doesn't add value?" The answer is self-evident, but if you need proof, then the earlier cited research bears' testament to the fact that substantial value is added to the business through business processes not measured by our Accounting Model. As we only manage what we measure, a failure to measure is a failure to manage.

As a highly exclusive measurement standard, the Accounting Model does not provide us with an appropriate measurement base, but if we dig a little deeper, the situation worsens...

c. What is profit? Profit is the value you add to your financial capital. So, profit is a value creation process. The objective of all business processes should be to add value; businesses are only successful when they add value to what they already have! Value creation is, therefore, the common purpose of all business processes, and so, from this, we can deduce that value creation is the common denominator of business. Consequently, as the common denominator, we can use value creation criteria to measure every business process, but we can't do the same using financial criteria. Until all business processes are incorporated into the mainstream of business measurement and management, we will not get a true reflection of business performance and underlying value. Business functions as a cause-and-effect model; all business components are interrelated in this causal model. As value creation is the common denominator of business, we can infer that business operates as a value creation causal model. We need to understand this model to measure and manage business effectively. No degree of adaptation or tweaking will help the Accounting Model; it's fundamentally not suited to measure and manage the value creation process. And as profit is a value creation process, or put differently, "value creation is the source of all profit", the profit objective is best served through measuring and managing the value creation process.

2. It masks value creation activities, hindering long-term growth.

What's the relationship, if any, between financial profit and value creation? We all know it's possible to make a financial profit yet destroy value, and we also know it's possible to create underlying value yet show a financial loss. So, from this, we can conclude that there is no correlation between financial profit and value creation. Financial profit masks our value creation activities, yet it is these value creation activities which build underlying business value, that supports and sustains future profit. So while it's important that we measure financial performance, it's equally important that we measure value creation activities, unless we want to be "led up the garden path" by our financials. Financial measures need to be incorporated into the value creation process because without the two, we are "flying blind." Financial and value creation measures are as different as chalk and cheese. One deals in pounds and pence and the other in probabilities and relationships. Financial measures are exclusive, short-term orientated and backwards-looking, whereas value creation measures are fully inclusive, long-term and forward-looking. Therefore, you cannot use a single model (e.g. the Accounting Model) and hope to get an accurate picture of business performance; you need an integrated model based on the value creation causal model. Our primary focus must be on the value creation processes - the true profit driver!

3. It measures inappropriate things and ignores important contributors.

The Accounting Model never set out to explain "how to play the game but only how to keep the financial score," so it's totally inadequate in even identifying, let alone ascribing value to critical value creation components within the business. Consider how the Accounting Model ascribes value to the business (or what it calls "book value"), which is made up of such things as property, machinery, tables and chairs, etc. Yet the most valuable assets, which drive value creation, are absent, such as:

- Ability to create or influence market demand.
- Ability to meet demand.
- Ability to optimise demand.
- Supply Chain opportunities.
- Staff skills, knowledge and motivation, etc. etc.

Inappropriate and inadequate financial measures have resulted in the huge chasm that has developed between book and market value. According to research (cited earlier), in the early 1980s, a company's book value compared to its market value was approximately 60 per cent. In the late 1990s, this had fallen to only 25 per cent and has now levelled out at between 15 and 20%, dependent on business type.

Apart from excluding critical value (wealth) creating assets, the Accounting Model ignores the cost of equity capital, and yet, this is often more significant than debt capital. It also ignores risk and changes to it. This is understandable as it is a backwards-looking measure, which can shed little light on risk, which is a "forward-looking interpretation of threats." In highly competitive markets, faced with constant change, risk assessment becomes even more critical. Poor information equals high risk.

4. It has a negative effect on economic growth.
It may be difficult to appreciate that a measurement model that's been with us for hundreds of years and used extensively by all of us and accepted by most as being "the language of business", is, in fact, potentially a wealth inhibitor or destroyer; but the facts are clear enough.

Responsible for a deteriorating risk / return investment profile.
As the Accounting Model cannot provide investors with sufficient and useful information upon which to base their investment decisions, they are at greater risk of ineffectively directing resources in our economy. The risk/return profile of investments has changed for the worst and is deteriorating as measurement standards have not changed to meet the needs of fiercely competitive and rapidly changing markets. Investment risk has, therefore, increased (as full knowledge and understanding of the investment are unknown) without an appropriate increase in return.

Successful investors are those who supplement financials with sound market knowledge or "gut feel." We thus become reliant on the abilities of a few rather than on an effective and universally accepted model to guide and assist all of us in the evaluation and investment process. Reliance on a few is only good for the few, not the wider economy.

When considering the investment issue, we must not overlook the enormous difficulties facing management in making internal investment decisions. On what basis does management decide to invest in the so-called "Accounting Intangibles," which make up more than eighty per cent of business value? Financial measures can only be used to evaluate financial results; they cannot tell you where we should invest, which is the most important decision of all. Without a method for quantifiably identifying investment opportunities within the murky depths of the "intangibles", the probabilities of investing in the wrong projects increases substantially.

Impedes economic growth.

As our primary measurement model, the Accounting Model's negative influence extends further than the potential for inappropriately directing resources. What you measure is what you get - so by using the Accounting Model to measure business performance, we encourage "strong financials," often at the expense of the value creators (which are not represented in the Accounting Model.) As managers are evaluated against their financials, they are not incentivised to invest in long-term wealth creating opportunities, because the more they invest in long-term value creators, the lower the book value of the business in the short-term. The Accounting Model, therefore, incentivises management to impede value creation and hinder economic growth. Short-term earnings at the expense of long-term sustainability benefit few!

Outlays on R&D (Research & Development) represent investments in potential new income streams, which should generate revenue well into the future. However, the Accounting Model treats them as worthless by expensing them. In effect, it takes the R & D asset and discards it. R & D is an asset as it enables the creation of income (i.e. it has value). The more you invest in R & D, the less profitable your business appears. The same applies to marketing costs invested in establishing brands, entering new markets, or gaining market share. All these outlays are investments to acquire new customers that should generate revenue well into the future, yet our Accounting Model expenses these outlays. Management is "incentivised" to cut back on potentially profitable marketing programmes and R&D just to make quarterly earnings look good!

The short-term tenure of senior managers encourages some of them to cut costs "below the bone" and to shun medium too long-term investment opportunities to further their own objectives. In some instances, figures are even manipulated to "improve earnings." The extent of this practice is unknown, yet it is believed to be prevalent. Ironically, the investment community have been "caught out" by a process they helped foster, namely, their obsession with quarterly earnings. In Chapter Four, I explained how professional managers (the executive) become proxy owners for shareholders, and how they are driven to produce short-term profits and dividends to please their paymasters. This is done by cutting back on investing in value creation projects and asset stripping. This leaves the business progressively weaker year-on-year. The long-term longevity of the business is placed at risk. This helps explain why business longevity is in decline.

Misdirects critical, finite resources.
The consequence of being unable to determine accurately business performance and underlying value, together with a short-term profit focus, means critical, finite resources (i.e. financial, people, materials and the environment) are being ineffectively employed in our economy; scarce resources are being ineffectively directed.

As our economy is the "engine room" of society, if we get our measurement standards wrong we will continue to misdirect scarce resources, which will reverberate throughout society, to the detriment of all.

Financial data can be highly misleading.
We live in a world of constant change; what relevance can you ascribe to myopic, one-sided, historical financial data? It makes no reference to future trends and the business's ability to survive, let alone prosper. Just how misleading is its data as it shows no, or very little, relation to market trends? For example, assets assumed to be important in the creation of wealth may be the complete opposite as their relevance to the market is unknown. An example could be finished stock that becomes obsolete

because of market changes and can only be sold as scrap. What appeared to be a financial asset is, in reality, a liability.

Over the past two decades, we have seen the fortunes of big and small businesses slide as a result of "strong financials" belying market realities. In fact, any business blindly pursuing the Accounting Model is courting disaster. If decisions are based on managing less than twenty per cent of the business, which the Accounting Model "manages", then the chances of making the wrong decisions are high! Poor information equals high risk.

Helps promote boardroom and strategic bias.

The dominance of the Accounting Model has led to another disturbing phenomenon. Boards are predominantly composed of those with financial backgrounds, to the exclusion of those with marketing backgrounds. Why has marketing always been under-represented on boards across all sectors, given the obvious importance of marketing?

The answer is rather simple; marketers are too a large extent involved in the process of value creation, and as the Accounting Model is inappropriate for measuring value creation activities, so marketing has been marginalised as their performance cannot be fully evaluated in financial terms. Their apparent lack of "accountability" has forced them out of boardrooms. This narrow financial perspective is inhibiting marketing from contributing to the future direction and strategy of their organisation to their organisation's and economy's detriment.

Dominates all other measures.

This is a critically important point. Let me explain - the inadequacies of our Accounting Model is nothing new; we have known about them for over three decades. Consequently, there have been some attempts to address these problems. Some of the more recent "solutions" are mentioned in Chapter One. There have been other models before them, such as the "Balanced Scorecard," some intangible asset measures and other lesser known, proprietary models/procedures have been trialled. There are many reasons why these "solutions" fall well short of meeting our requirements for a workable solution. The main reason being they don't meet our "two minimum requirements." Firstly they are not based on any understanding of the value creation causal model (our underlying business model.) Secondly, the measures are not comparable across all businesses irrespective of sector or size. This means the Accounting Model remains dominant because its measures are comparable, and comparability is critically important to our economy. Consequently, businesses ensure they produce strong financials, to remain attractive to external investors. Decisions are often taken in favour of "strong financials", even although the decision makers may feel their decisions favouring the Accounting Model to be counterintuitive. Any measurement system, which is incomparable, will operate under the shadow of the Accounting Model and therefore, will never achieve its full potential. Like a small tree, living under the canopy of a giant in the forest has little chance of survival, unless the giant topples. Without comparable measures, any alternative measure will be dominated by our Accounting Model. Because of this dominance, soon it makes little sense following the alternate measurement system. That's why The Balanced Scorecard and all others have lost ground, and are almost defunct, despite the Balanced Scorecard offering a better alternative than financials alone.

5. Supports a "profiteering" approach
Profiteering is defined as using an "unfair advantage" to profit from another - that is, to charge a higher price, or pay a lower price, using some unfair advantage to do so. A measurement standard which only favours shareholder interests over all other stakeholders (those involved in the business to try and make it successful) definitely qualifies as an unfair advantage. Let's look at some of these unfair practices.

To ensure a business produces strong financials (its measure of success,) the business decides not to increase salaries/wages in-line with inflation. Neither does it undertake adequate staff training/development, despite it acknowledging its benefits. They actively discourage staff from joining trade unions to limit labours collective bargaining. They employ locally trained staff but do nothing to support local training/educational institutions. Further, they introduce manufacturing processes which are harmful to the environment but are more profitable. They also extend creditor payments to reduce their bank overdraft, to fund their business, to increase their profit. The list of activities they undertake to improve profits at the expense of stakeholders goes on and on. As stakeholder interests are not part of our measurement standard, they are not effectively managed - this is the unfair advantage. They take from their stakeholders to make their financials look good, so shareholders may benefit. They rob Peter to Pay Paul. This is blatant profiteering.

What's more, it's the worst form of profiteering imaginable. They are taking from the people who are working with them to try and make them successful. It's like robbing your own family - the people you should be protecting and helping - it's disgusting. Profiteering is bad enough, where businesses use an unfair advantage over others not associated with them, but to do it to those closest to you is inexcusable.

Of course, business faces conflicting interests in deciding whom to reward and by how much. However, when all the conflicting interests are considered in terms of their interrelationships and overall impact (based on the value creation causal model) one can make an informed decision on who and how much to reward conflicting interests. Ignoring them and rewarding one, sets the business up to fail. Soon those excluded from consideration will withhold their support, and it will become increasingly difficult to succeed. Another reason business longevity is in decline.

6. Promotes inequality within society.

Reliance on a single, biased measurement standard has created an adversarial form of management where almost all decisions are judged in favour of short-term profit considerations. In so doing, we have established a win / lose relationship, where invariably, short-term profit "wins" as this is what business is measured and evaluated against. As a result, customers, suppliers, staff, stakeholders (i.e. wider society) and the environment are seen as "adversaries." Short-term profit gained at the expense of these "adversaries" is the objective of the Accounting Model. Its objective is to maximise profit and retain the proceeds for shareholders. Consequently, wealth is "hoarded" by an exclusive few; not evenly distributed within society. Poor distribution of wealth is not beneficial to the wider economy and society. According to recent research, 85 of the wealthiest people own more wealth than approximately 3.5 billion of the poorest people. There are so many statistics on the rich/poor divide, it's hard for people not to know of it and that it's getting worse rapidly. The major contributor is our inadequate and inappropriate business measurement standard.

In contrast, a long-term value creation perspective sees all participants in business as critical partners in the process of value creation. It realises that sustained, long-term profitability is only achieved through mutual benefit. As a consequence, wealth is not hoarded but rather spread, to create a more viable future for all. This has enormous socio-economic and environmental advantages. Fairness is built into the measures so we won't require archaic post-redistribution mechanisms to distribute wealth/value. It also prevents bad business practices being used in the first place.

7. It provides limited management measures.
To be fair to our Accounting Model - it's perfectly good at measuring financial results, the task for which it was developed. We can hardly blame it for any inadequacies in measuring tasks it was not intended for when introduced over 500 years ago. When change is limited, past performance is useful in predicting the future, but today change is rapid, relentless and widespread. Our focus has to be on the future. We have to anticipate and respond to the dynamics of our rapidly changing markets. We cannot use the Accounting Model for this purpose. We have to understand and measure the value creation processes to give us a clear insight into possible future performance.

Consequently, we need to expand our measurement standard to incorporate the heart of business, or how a business creates value. We still need to record what has happened in business regarding financial transactions, but it cannot remain our sole and dominant business measure. It will have to become part of a wider set of measurement standards, which will provide a more balanced view of business performance, its underlying value and how well placed it is to perform in the future.

Business has changed considerably over the past five hundred years since the introduction of the Accounting Model; don't you think its time our measurement standard followed suit? We don't have any option - the situation is dire. We need a completely different approach to measuring and managing business. We need to focus on, and manage value within business - we need a new measurement standard, and we need it now.

The biggest change we can ever make!

By now, you will have realised that the biggest change we can make to society, environment, business and the economy is to change our business measurement standard. It will positively impact all facets of life. Nothing can be bigger.

Index

Index

Index

www.ingramcontent.com/pod-product-compliance
Lightning Source LLC
Chambersburg PA
CBHW020202200326
41521CB00005BA/221